BASKETRY

BASKETRY
Projects from Baskets to Grass Slippers

Hisako Sekijima

Foreword by
Jack Lenor Larsen

Photographs by
Akihiko Tokue

KODANSHA INTERNATIONAL
Tokyo • New York • London

for my husband

Acknowledgments:
I owe too much to too many persons to list all of their names here, but I would like to express my great appreciation for their help. I especially would like to thank my first teacher, Akimichi Hashimoto; Ed Rossbach and John McQueen, who led me to contemporary basketry; Carol G. Hart, Sandra Newman, Ken and Kathleen Dalton, and Shoji Sugawara, who imparted their traditional know-how; and Illy Valyi, Bob Hanson, Barbara Stephan, Masa Kinoshita, and Joanne S. Brandford, who advised and helped me in various ways. I also would like to thank my husband Yasuo for his true understanding and valuable opinion, and my parents for raising plants for me.

This book would never have been completed without my editors, Michiko Uchiyama and Rowena Wildin of Kodansha International, who checked the draft of my manuscript and turned the ambiguous into the precise. I would like to extend my endless appreciation for their excellent editorial work.

Photo credits:
Bob Hanson, p. 8; Tadao Tominari, pp. 46—47 (bamboo, willow, paper mulberry, wisteria, sinomenine).

Drawings by Eiko Ikeda.

The publisher would like to thank the following for their assistance: Gallery Tomoe-do, Masuda Studio Gallery, and Mr. Masaki Nakayama of Konchū-kan, Yukari no Mori.

Distributed in the United States by Kodansha America, Inc., 114 Fifth Avenue, New York, NY 10011.

Published by Kodansha International Ltd., 17-14, Otowa 1-chome, Bunkyo-ku, Tokyo 112 and Kodansha America, Inc.

Library of Congress Cataloging-in-Publication Data
Sekijima, Hisako.
    Basketry: projects from baskets to grass slippers.
    Bibliography: p.
    Includes index.
    1. Basket making.   1. Title.
TT879.B3S45   1986   746.41'2   85-45707
ISBN 4-7700-1525-9

Contents

Foreword by Jack Lenor Larsen 6

Introduction 8

BASKETRY BASICS 9

Interplay of Form, Material, and Method 10
1. Analysis of a basket 15
2. Woven basket 17
3. Twined openwork basket 25
4. Coiled basket 33
5. Plaited basket 37

The Properties and Preparation of Materials 44
Interaction of materials and methods 48
6. How to prepare paper mulberry bark 50
7. How to prepare cherry bark 52
8. How to split bamboo stalks 54
9. How to split a maple log 57
10. How to make twine and braid 60
11. Dyeing with onion skins 65

BASKETRY CONCEPTS ON THE MOVE 67

DIFFERENT PERSPECTIVES 77

LEARNING FROM NATURE 78
12. Hanging basket made from windmill palm stem 79

FROM A TWO-DIMENSIONAL PLANE TO A THREE-DIMENSIONAL FORM 82
13. Hanging basket with curved bottom 83
14. Japanese winnowing basket 88

RESPONDING TO THE PROPERTIES OF MATERIALS 96
15. Cattail braid and maple splint basket 97
16. Short-strand coiled mat 101

DEVICES THAT MAKE THINGS POSSIBLE AND EASIER 109
17. Plaited basket in a free-form willow basket 110
18. Bamboo screen with weighted bobbin twining 115
19. Grass slippers 119

ANOTHER ASPECT OF TRADITIONAL TECHNIQUES 126
20. A string of peppers 127
21. Rice cakes wrapped in dwarf bamboo leaves 130
22. Protective snow cap for plants 133
23. Wrapped eggs 137

Personal interest in sources of material 140

For your reference 141
Tools 141
Places to see baskets 142
Selected publications 142

Index 144

Foreword

This publication of Hisako Sekijima's *Basketry* will prove to be as pertinent as it is timely. The current rush towards basketmaking as a craft and as an art form, as a subject of collections and publications, has not, heretofore, been accompanied by serious consideration of how to achieve skills in basketry techniques. Those few books in print tend to be slight volumes directed to the very young. *Interlacing: The Elemental Fabric*, although ambitious in the breadth and depth of its coverage, is not concerned with *making*. In that sense, *Basketry* is complementary to it.

When my generation attended college, basketmaking was the mythic "snap course." Such is not the case; even for weavers with dexterity and a fine sense of organization, the preparation and manipulation of basketry materials is an *acquired* skill, passed down from master to novice.

Sekijima brings to this task some paramount attributes. First, she became a master of her craft, understanding both its oriental and western aspects. As a teacher she is a born natural, intent on organizing material to be readily perceived—without inhibiting the student's sensitivities. Unlike most Japanese writing in English, Sekijima's prose flows so easily as to make the comprehension of all of this "a piece of cake." Through the step-by-step drawings and their comprehensible descriptions our confidence grows. This, incidentally, is not typical of existing treatises on basketmaking. Usually made by a third party, the drawings are often inaccurate and their descriptions befuddling.

That Hisako Sekijima so easily conveys an understanding of East and West brings me to my next point. In spite of its objectivity, her book is a personal one—appropriately sauced with her perception of natural laws. That our exposure to the Japanese view of nature and the interpenetration of perceiving and creating comes from a young contemporary, knowledgeable of the West, makes this volume valuable as a bridge to traditions and thought processes so foreign as to remain vague—even to this Japanophile. Her thought processes as she approaches a broad spectrum of materials, techniques and projects, reveals these sensitivities in a language quite available to the reader.

As for basketry, why so important now? The response must be its success as an anecdote to a visual and sensual impoverishment deeply affecting the modern psyche. Both the spaces built today and the objects within them are without a sense of materials or structure. More adhesive than cohesive, they fail to satisfy our innate need to identify with reality—to know within our bones what things are—and how they came to be that way. Whether in mats or containers, basketry expresses both materials and structures more perceptibly than do textiles. Basketry reaffirms the fibrous condition mankind was born into. Because nature IS the fiber of grasses and trees, as well as the tissues and sinews of our own bodies, we relate to it. Too far removed from fiber, we do not relate at all.

Because basketry traditions still remain in many parts of the world and are, in fact, the most successful craft export of developing nations, many of us collect baskets. But the pleasure of making them! The acquired skills, the understanding of materials and the orders of interlacing, being in control of matter, resolving problems, self expression —isn't this exactly what we crave today?

Then too, we find a link to our remote past. Anthropologists working on the traces of our earliest ancestors are now convinced that they were not hunters but gatherer-scavengers, and that their invention of the basket became the most pivotal of tools. Baskets made it possible to join together for shared meals instead of eating "on the spot" as animals do. This in turn led to language, development of the brain, and, in more permanent baskets, man's first system. Out of this developed mathematics on one hand, yarn spinning and woven fabrics on the other.

But the loom, however useful in quickly making a consistently uniform fabric, greatly limits the craftsman. In basketry there remains the option for working compound curves and complex shapes in the full three dimensions—with the widest range of materials and applications. And, while textiles tend to be a raw material for a cutting and sewing process, basketry produces finished forms, ready for use or quiet contemplation. Chances for personal expression are here. So is the potential for making art.

Jack Lenor Larsen

Introduction

Untitled.
Private collection.
Akebia; interlaced; 10″ (25.5 cm);
1979.
Photo by Bob Hanson.

I tried to make the basket shown here without using any conventional construction methods. Making it turned the direction of my basketmaking away from technical concerns. This attempt was the result of studying at a workshop given by John McQueen at Peter's Valley Craft Center in New Jersey in 1978. I had also been influenced by Ed Rossbach's book *Baskets as Textile Art* and the conceptual basketry work of several artists in the United States, where I lived for several years while my husband was assigned to his company's New York office.

I found that the basket I created successfully represented my definition of basketry and my preference for using materials naturally. Not only had I departed from designing modifications of conventional techniques, but I had also found a new dimension of expressive potential in basketry and its materials. Instead of building a woven wall out of tangible material, I gave equal value to the interior space and the spaces in the textile structure. Natural materials became more than a physical medium with which to visualize my idea. As soon as I stopped forcing materials into a predesigned form and let natural materials transform themselves, I found the inherent properties were more effectively revealed. Thus I turned all "restrictions" derived from material and method into a means of conceptualizing baskets. Now I try to match the form that the properties of the material suggest with the form that results from my conceptualizing.

When we create new baskets, we tend either to completely disregard tradition or to seek out unusual techniques, old or contemporary, used by skillful craftsmen. To be creative, however, does not mean to simply combine various methods and techniques. The basketmaker must have his own standpoint from which to reevaluate others. He must understand the impact of techniques and methods in his own terms. Then it is possible to create new baskets that provide a natural connection between the basketmaker's sensitivity and historical and more universal aesthetic values.

Throughout the book, I have emphasized building new ideas based on the individual's personal interpretation and practical modification of basketmaking traditions. In one sense, this book is a record of my gradual understanding of the medium through the experimental basketry I have been doing in my studio from the first early attempts to the present.

This book gives step-by-step instructions for each project. The purpose of these instructions is not to remove all the rough stones from your path, but to enable you to overcome these difficulties and to prepare you to go beyond the security of what you are already familiar with. These projects have been designed and arranged to demonstrate how expanding an idea can create new forms, and to teach you the basics of basketry. Equal emphasis has been placed on the overall discussion of basketry basics and on the projects themselves.

BASKETRY BASICS

Rather than presenting a survey of traditional construction
methods and hard-and-fast rules for preparing and using
materials, I have tried to discover what lies behind the rules
and traditions. My analysis of the basic aspects of basketry
examines the interplay of material and method with the
form of the finished basket.

Interplay of Form, Material, and Method

I had a chance to examine a weaverbird's nest last summer. It looked like a grayish green ball of narrow silk ribbon and fit comfortably in the palm of my hand. I was told that weaverbirds build a nest by a much more complex method than simply piling blades of grass on top of each other. They make a foundation for the nest by wrapping long blades of grass, usually of the genus *Cyperus* around a forked tree branch. Then they construct a perching ring, which hangs down vertically, around the foundation. While resting on the ring, they use their beaks to weave hundreds of blades under and over each other, forming an almost spherical shape.

weaverbird on its nest

Textile technology includes not only loom weaving of cloth, but also a variety of methods that do not use any machinery and resemble those used by the weaverbirds. Nonloom, or off-loom, techniques include netting, macrame, sprang, knitting, braiding, lace making, crocheting, basketry, bag making, and mat making. These techniques are named after the finished product and are usually considered separate categories. However, these different methods actually share many forms and methods. For instance, the so-called "twined form" is found in basketry, braiding, mat making, screen making, and even in architecture. If emphasis is placed on the similarity of method and form rather than the different final products, these off-loom techniques can be seen as one large category. Thus, instead of limiting basketry to the methods used in making traditional container baskets, it can include all off-loom techniques used to construct a three-dimensional object out of fibrous materials.

Through the years man has developed ways to improve the properties of fibrous materials by plying slender stems of grasses into sturdier and longer ropes or by fashioning them into mats or baskets. No matter what means is used, the pliability or resilence of the raw material will determine whether it becomes a connecting or supporting element both during the process of construction and in the resulting structure. Manipulation of the material by twisting or bending it amplifies the inherent resilience of the material and allows it to sustain a physical balance among the components. The total of the balanced forces creates and sustains the entire form of the object. In three-dimensional objects like baskets, there is an interplay of form, material, and method that gives them both a textile and a sculptural quality. In each basket, it determines the texture, movement of lines, rhythm of interworking fibers, and tension among components, all characteristics of textiles. At the same time, this interplay influences the relation of lines and planes, the contrast of shadow and light on the angled planes, multidimensional involvement of space, and balance of resilient elements, all characteristics of sculpture or architecture.

In basketry, certain basic forms are transformed into more complex shapes technically or as a result of individual creativity. I have classified basketry methods into six basic types to show how the primary parts are altered with the addition of transformational factors. An understanding of the relationship between these basic methods and derivative factors will help the basketmaker analyze any variants and use his analysis and interpretation of the technical and personal forces acting on a basket to create new forms.

I used the following structural characteristics to analyze basketry techniques.

A. Functional equality of materials
   1. A single, homogeneous material is the structural unit and supports the entire form.
   2. Two or more components with different strengths have different structural functions. That is, stronger components play a supporting role, and weaker ones act as connectors.
B. Number and function of interworking components
   1. A single component interworks with itself.
   2. One set of components works as a group in a mutually transferable manner.
   3. Two or more sets of components have respective functions—binder/foundation, warp/weft, warp/a set of wefts.
C. Property of component as it contributes to the structure
   1. Pliable
   2. Resilient
   3. Combination of pliable and resilient components
   4. Combination of resilient and less resilient components
D. Movement causing resilience
   1. Circling
   2. Under/over
   3. Combination of circling and under/over movements
E. Interworking of components
   1. Looped
   2. Knotted
   3. Interlaced at a fixed angle
   4. Bound, connected, and coiled
   5. Woven
   6. Woven and twisted together
F. Angular relation between the direction of interworking and that of growth of plane
   1. Right angle
   2. Parallel
   3. Oblique

STRUCTURAL CHARACTERISTICS	A	homogeneous		different		
	B	single	one set of two or more	two or more sets		
				binder/foundation	warp/weft	warp/set of wefts
	C	pliable	resilient	pliable & resilient	resilient & less so	resilient & less so, or pliable
	D	circling	under/over	circling	under/over	circling & under/over
	E	looped	knotted	interlaced at a fixed angle	bound, connected, & coiled	woven	woven & twisted together
	F	right angle	parallel	oblique	right angle		
BASIC METHODS		LOOPING	KNOTTING	PLAITING	COILING	WEAVING	TWINING

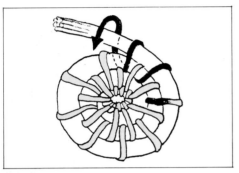

LOOPING: A single component interworks with itself in continuous loops one after another; each new loop is worked on the previous loop and/or a loop from a previous row.

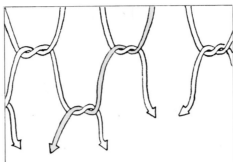

KNOTTING: Multiple components are linked; intersections are secured by knots.

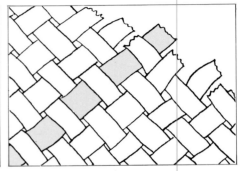

PLAITING: Multiple components are interlaced at a fixed angle by a certain rhythm of under/over alternation, and the points of intersection are secured by the resilient force of the material.

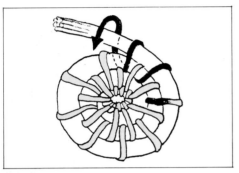

COILING: The continuous foundation coils around in a spiral; each new round is bound and connected to the previous one by a more pliable component.

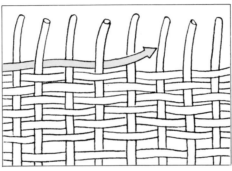

WEAVING: The resilient warps are interlaced with a less resilient weft in an alternating under/over rhythm.

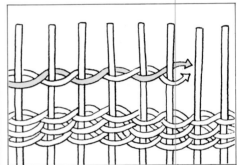

TWINING: The resilient warps are connected by a pair of pliable wefts twisted together.

When structural characteristics are used to analyze basketry techniques, six basic methods become evident. Projects 2 through 5 are examples of some of these.

When these six basic methods are combined with the following transformational factors, more complex structures are possible and the creative potential of basketry is revealed.

Factors related to the property of the material: flexibility, resilience, thickness, width, shape of cut-end, smoothness of surface, tightness of ply.

Factors related to structural components: even or odd number of components, manner or rhythm of interworking, frequency of intersection.

Factors related to manipulation methods: tightness of pulling, twisting, or bending; frequency of repetition; direction of manipulation.

Factors related to decorative and other elements: overlaying, embroidery, dyeing, painting, attaching.

A careful examination of these transformational factors reveals that they are essentially the same interplay of form, material, and method. Actual baskets are often mixtures of different basic methods and several transformational factors. These six examples illustrate the relationship.

"Cut and opened hull." Vine is looped at center in a crochetlike manner. It is made of inter-looped layers of loops.

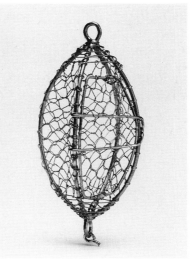

Netted bait sinker. Sets of four components are knotted.

Japanese splint basket. Plaited in an under-two/over-two pattern at a right angle.

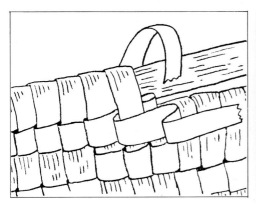

Detail of imbricated basket. In this technique, often found in American Indian and African baskets, a flat, tapelike material is overlaid, folded, and bound every row of the coil.

"Indented." An even number of flat warps of maple splints are woven with a weft row of cattail braid and then one of vine. This technique is called "chasing."

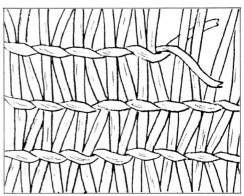

Detail of twining. Paired warps are twined. Each warp strand is paired with the strand to its right in one row and then with the strand to the left in the next row. Openwork is created if resilient material is used for warps and wefts.

		LOOPING	KNOTTING	PLAITING	COILING	WEAVING	TWINING
STRUCTURAL CHARACTERISTICS	A	homogeneous			different		
	B	single	one set of two or more		two or more sets		
					binder/foundation	warp/weft	warp/set of wefts
	C	pliable		resilient	pliable & resilient	resilient & less so	resilient & less so, or pliable
	D	circling		under/over	circling	under/over	circling & under/over
	E	looped	knotted	interlaced at a fixed angle	bound, connected, & coiled	woven	woven & twisted together
	F	right angle	parallel	oblique	right angle		
BASIC METHODS		LOOPING	KNOTTING	PLAITING	COILING	WEAVING	TWINING
EXAMPLES		"Cut and opened hull"	Netted bait sinker	Japanese splint basket	Detail of imbrication	"Indented"	Detail of twining
TRANSFORMATIONAL FACTORS	MATERIAL	—pliable, but very springy —round	—pliable metal wire —retains shape	—very flexible —thin and flat	—flat binder	—flat warp —wide thick weft and round linear weft	—warp and weft have almost identical properties
	STRUCTURE	—looped at the middle like crochet	—several sets of two —increase the number of sets	—increase and decrease of the number of sets —under-2/over-2 rhythm	—rows connected to previous rows with binding strand	—even number of warps —chasing one weft after the other	—paired warps —changing pairs —each row forms zigzag
	METHOD	—crochet over crocheted structure	—linked two times —done over a framework	—plaited tightly	—densely coiled		
	OTHERS	—finished shell is clipped open		—overlay of cherry bark at corners (also serves as reinforcement)	—overlay of flat material	—cattail braided in advance	—coloring part of warps

ANALYSIS OF A BASKET

Analyzing examples of basketry reveals that all baskets are just combinations of the six basic methods and transformational factors, however complicated they may look at first glance. Use this knowledge to help you identify the structure and construction methods of a finished basket. Once you have grasped the basic method and determined how the transformational factors give it complexity, you will be able to make a similar basket or use the techniques in a basket of your own design.

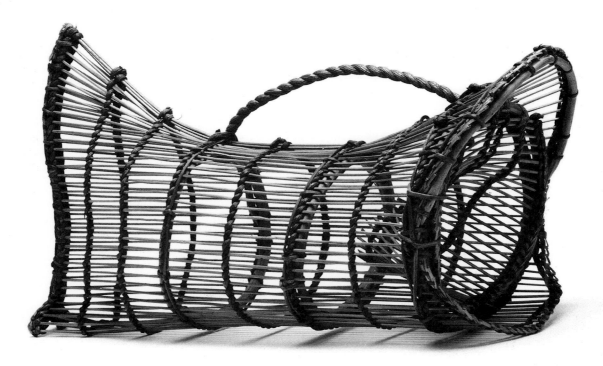

BASKET TO BE ANALYZED: A replica of a fish trap that I am told is used in Malawi, southeastern Africa.
H 7½″ (19 cm) × W 6″ (15 cm) × D 14″ (35.5 cm)

As you examine the five photos of the fish trap, ask yourself these questions.
The answers to the questions follow in chart form.

1. What techniques have been used? Bending, folding, tying, wrapping, looping, knotting, twining, plaiting, coiling, weaving?
2. Which of these techniques is dominant in the body of the basket?
3. How was the funnel-shaped trap mouth made?

4. How many different types of materials can you recognize? What are their functions?
5. How was the horn shape widened?
6. How are the borders finished off?
7. What is the most interesting feature?

BASIC METHODS	TRANSFORMATIONAL FACTORS		
	MATERIAL	STRUCTURE	METHOD
LOOPING	**Q4:** Fine split vine is looped around.	**Q1:** Vine is looped around spokes and large supporting rod, holds tail flat.	**Q7:** Cylindrical form is pushed flat at the tail.
KNOTTING	**Q1:** Vine ends are knotted.		
PLAITING	**Q4:** Spokes are thinned where bent at borders.	**Q6:** Thinned spokes are plaited to make the border.	
COILING			
WEAVING			
TWINING	**Q4:** Spokes are fine palm splits; twining strands and reinforcing rods are thicker splits of vine. **Q7:** Spokes look finer than twining strands.	**Q2:** Main body is twined. **Q3:** Funnel part is twined back and forth. **Q5:** Number of spokes is increased to open the twined horn shape and tail.	**Q7:** Twined rows spaced to create openwork.

2

WOVEN BASKET

When I follow conventional techniques, it gives me a feeling of security very different from the excitement I feel when I am experimenting with new techniques and creating baskets that are personal expressions. We tend to simply ignore rules and conventions because we feel they are too restrictive, but studying the reasons behind these rules helps us appreciate how carefully they have been thought out and developed in response to certain situations. Almost every problem has been anticipated and covered in the rules. Use this security as a base from which to develop your sensitivity.

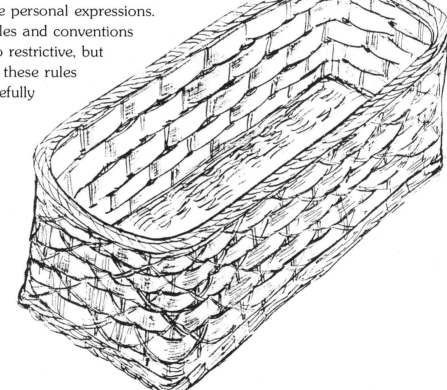

MATERIALS

1 oz (30 gm) of 1/32″ (1 mm) #0 round reed
See step 1 for how to estimate the necessary amount.
Soak for 5 to 10 minutes.

2½″ (6.5 cm) × 30″ (76 cm) strips of cherry bark
See Project 7, page 52.
See step 18 for how to estimate the necessary amount.
Soak for 2 to 3 hours.

FINISHED SIZE:
H 3½″ (9 cm) × W 5½″ (14 cm) × L 10¼″ (26 cm)

EQUIPMENT

Flower arrangement shears
Single-edged knife
Needle-nosed pliers
Awl
Alcohol burner or gas range burner
Clothespins
Board

INSTRUCTIONS

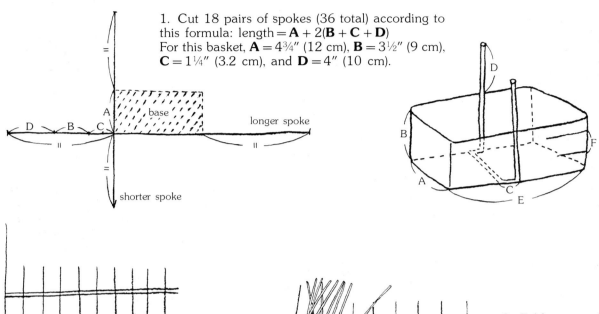

1. Cut 18 pairs of spokes (36 total) according to this formula: length = $A + 2(B + C + D)$
For this basket, $A = 4\frac{3}{4}''$ (12 cm), $B = 3\frac{1}{2}''$ (9 cm), $C = 1\frac{1}{4}''$ (3.2 cm), and $D = 4''$ (10 cm).

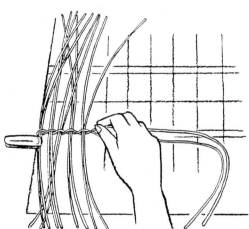

2. On your working board, draw the outline of the base of the basket with the long side horizontal. Mark the center of the short side and mark several vertical guide lines for weaving. Mark the twined border with two horizontal lines.

3. Fold a strand of round reed at least twice the length of the basket in half and begin twining the 18 pairs of vertical spokes starting at the lower left corner of the rectangle along the inner horizontal line. To twine, slip the twining strand around the leftmost pair of spokes, cross the strand with the front strand on top, insert another pair of spokes, cross the strands again, and repeat. After twining several pairs, secure the end to the board with a clothespin.

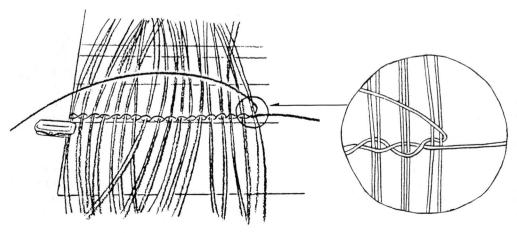

4. When all 18 pairs have been twined, bend one of the twining strands around the last pair and weave it under the next pair to the left and over the second pair to the left. Continue weaving this strand in an under-one/over-one pattern to the left end. The other twining strand will be cut off in step 10.

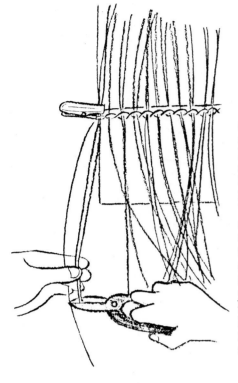

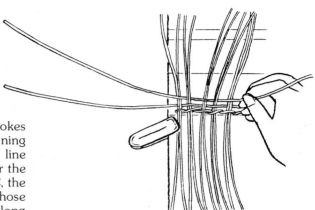

5. Adjust the length of the spokes above and below the first twining line. The spokes above the line should be long enough to cover the bottom **A**, the border twining **C**, the height **B**, and the border **D**; those below the line should be long enough to cover the border twining **C**, the height **B**, and the border **D** of the basket. The space between spokes should be about ½" (1.3 cm). Cut the twining strand that you have just woven in to the same length as the lower part of the vertical spokes. Move the clothespin if necessary. Place the cut end to the left of the work.

6. Working from the left side, weave a new strand above the woven single strand in an under-one/over-one pattern, alternating the under and over pattern with the strand below it.

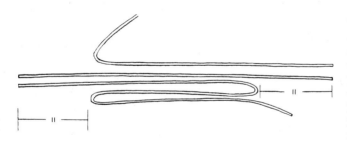

7. Match the cut end of the new strand with the cut end of the previous woven strand. These two strands make a pair of horizontal spokes on the left. Cut the right end of this spoke to the same length as the left end. Working from the right edge, weave in a new strand, matching its cut end with that of the previous row, forming a pair of horizontal spokes.

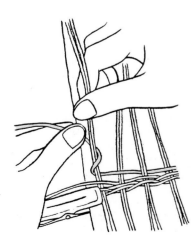

8. Weave to the left with this strand. When you come to the edge of the work, wrap the strand around the pair of spokes at the edge as shown to prevent the spokes on the edge from getting too close to the second pair from the edge. Weave back and forth for ½" (1.3 cm). Make another pair of horizontal spokes repeating steps 6 and 7.

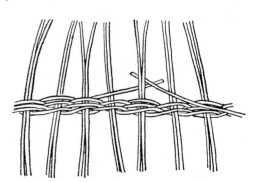

9. When the strand runs out in the middle, add a new one, crossing the ends of the old and new strands under a vertical pair of spokes. The next row of weaving will secure the joint.

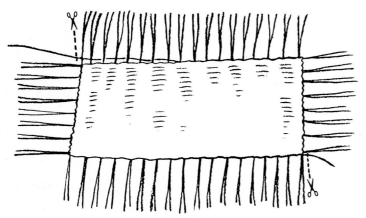

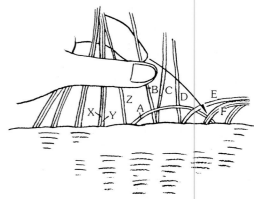

10. Continue weaving, leaving horizontal spokes at ½" (1.3 cm) intervals until there are eight pairs of horizontal spokes on each side. Cut off the last weaving strand and the first weaving strand (see step 4) at the edge of the work.

11. To make a twinelike band where the basket turns from the bottom to the side, bend all the spokes to the right one by one. Starting in the middle of the long side, bend spoke **A** (the right half of a pair) over **B**, **C**, and **D**, and insert it between **D** and **E**. Bend spoke **B** over **C**, **D**, and **E**, and insert it between **E** and **F**. The corners of the basket will be gently rounded. Continue all the way around the edge of the basket until you reach the third spoke from **A** (spoke **X**).

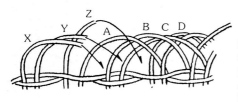

12. Bend **X** over **Y**, **Z**, and **A**, and insert it behind spoke **B**, which is already bent. Bend **Y** over the next three spokes and behind **C**; and **Z** over the next three spokes and behind **D**.

13. Turn the basket so the side that was facing you in steps 11 and 12 is on the bottom. All the bent spokes should be standing and leaning to the right.

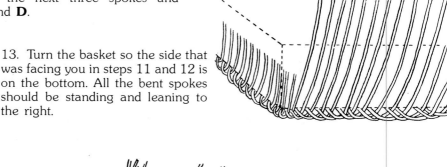

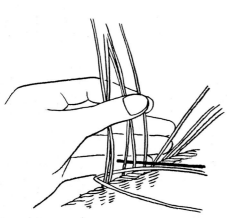

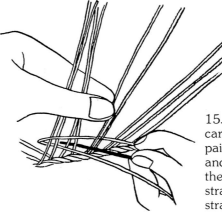

14. Bend a twining strand in half and put the looped end around any two spokes. Put another single strand behind the next two spokes. These three strands will be used to do a row of twining to pair the spokes and to make the spokes stand up straight.

15. To twine with three strands, carry the outer left strand over two pairs of spokes, behind the third pair, and to the front. Do the same with the other end of the folded twining strand and then with the inserted strand. Repeat.

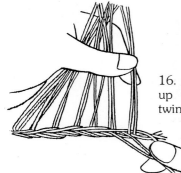

16. Try to pull the spokes straight up while you do the three-strand twining.

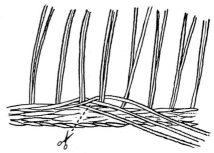

17. Make three rows of three-strand twining. Clip off the outer left strand.

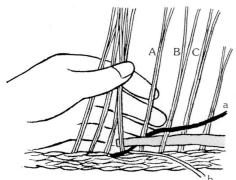

18. Cut the cherry bark according to these formulas: length grainwise = $2(\mathbf{A} + \mathbf{E})$, width = $\mathbf{F}$
For this basket, $\mathbf{E} = 10''$ (25.5 cm) and $\mathbf{F} = \frac{5}{8}''$ (1.5 cm). Place a strip of cherry bark between the two remaining strands. The outer left strand **b** should be in front of two pairs of spokes (**A** and **B**); the bark should be in front of the first pair **A**, behind the second **B**, and in front of the third **C**; the inner strand **a** should be behind the first pair of spokes **A** and in front of the second pair **B**, above the cherry bark.

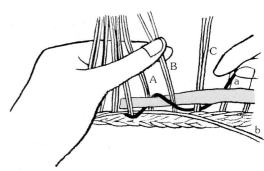

19. Pass strand **a** in front of spoke pair **B** and the cherry bark, behind spoke pair **C** and the cherry bark, and then in front of the next pair of spokes.

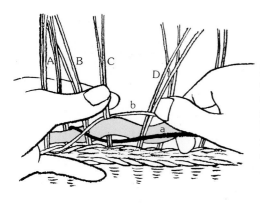

20. On top of spoke pair **B**, cross strand **b** over **a**. Pass strand **b** behind spoke pair **C** above the cherry bark and in front of spoke pair **D**. Put the strip of cherry bark behind spoke pair **D** and in front of the next pair of spokes. The strands and bark should always be in front of a pair of spokes when not being moved.

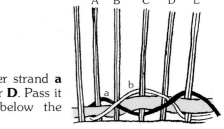

21. Cross strand **b** under strand **a** and in front of spoke pair **D**. Pass it behind spoke pair **E** below the cherry bark.

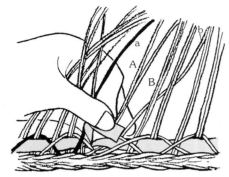

22. Continue in the same way. When you reach the end of the first row, cut the strip of cherry bark and tuck the cut end under spoke pair **B** (where the strands first cross).

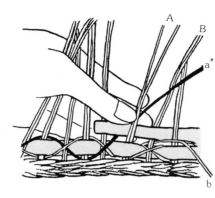

23. The two strands are not cut, but carried to the second row. Insert a new strip of cherry bark behind spoke pair **A**, over spoke pair **B**, and over strand **a**. In the second row, the crossed and uncrossed spokes are reversed.

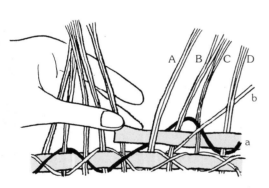

24. Slip strand **a** behind spoke pair **B**, in front of pair **C**, and under pair **D**, below the cherry bark. Cross strand **b** over **a** and pass **b** behind spoke pair **D** above the bark strip. Weave five rows in this diamond pattern.

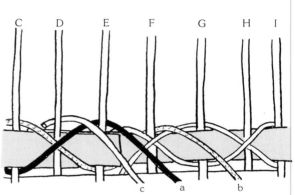

25. After the fifth row, do three rows of three-strand twining. Use strands **a** and **b** from the diamond pattern and add one more strand **c** behind spoke pair **D**. See step 15 for an explanation of three-strand twining.

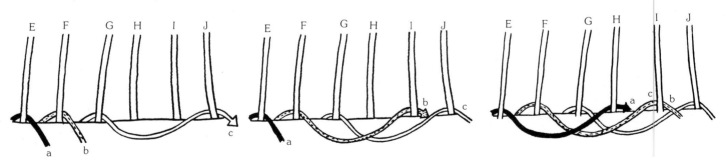

26. At the beginning of the third row of twining, instead of first passing strand **a** behind spoke pair **H**, start by passing strand **c** behind spoke pair **J**; then pass **b** behind **I**, and **a** behind **H**. This is the reverse of the normal working order. Finish the third row of twining in the normal working order.

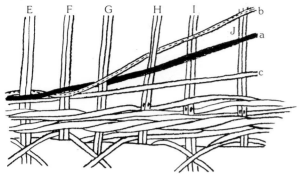

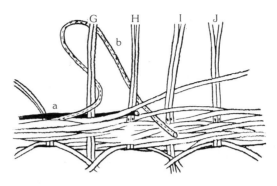

27. There should be three openings in the twining at spoke pairs **H**, **I**, and **J**.

28. Clip off strand **a** right after it passes in front of spoke pair **H**. Take the end of strand **b**, insert it under the top strand of twining between spoke pairs **H** and **I** and bring it to the front.

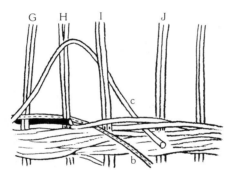

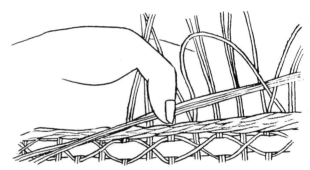

29. Pass strand **c** behind spoke pair **I**, insert it under the top two strands of twining between spoke pairs **I** and **J** and bring it to the front. Clip off strands **b** and **c** just after they cross spoke pairs **I** and **J** respectively. The openings made in the previous row have been filled with the ends of the three strands.

30. Thoroughly soak the spokes protruding from the twined edge. Make a bunch out of four strands of round reed and lay it over the spokes at their base, all the way around the basket. The round reeds will be the foundation for the border wrapping. Starting with any single spoke, bend it around the bunch of reeds and over the next five spokes. Insert the end of the spoke below the reeds and pull it to the inside of the basket.

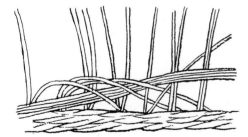

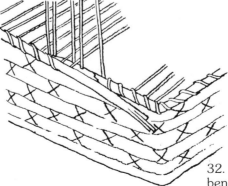

31. Continue this process with subsequent spokes until only five spokes remain. This process is the same as the one explained in steps 11 and 12 except that here it is done over a bunch of reeds.

32. See step 12 for how to finish bending the last five spokes.

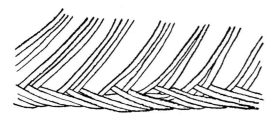

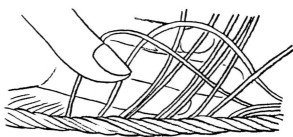

33. Finish the ends of the spokes that are now on the inside of the basket in the same way. This will form a twinelike border on the inside of the basket and will hide and secure the clipped ends of all the spokes.

34. Starting with any spoke, bend it over the next five spokes to the right and insert it between this spoke and the sixth one. Repeat until you have gone all the way around the basket, forming two rows of twinelike border.

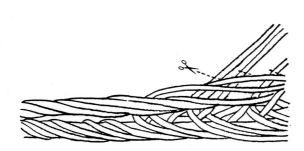

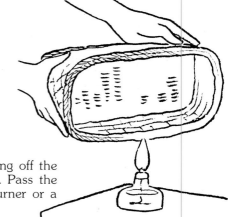

35. Clip off all the ends of the spokes.

36. Finish the basket by burning off the frayed ends of the round reed. Pass the basket over a small alcohol burner or a burner on a gas range.

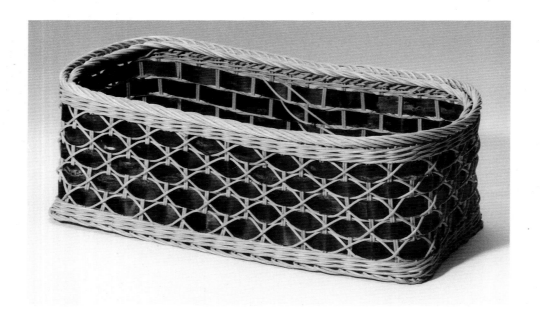

3

TWINED OPENWORK
BASKET

The twined structure consists of a
single warp and a pair of wefts. The
linear wefts of this tightly woven,
clothlike basket create lacey, strong
openwork, especially with the addition
of a horizontal rod called "ti"
in Pomo Indian basketry.

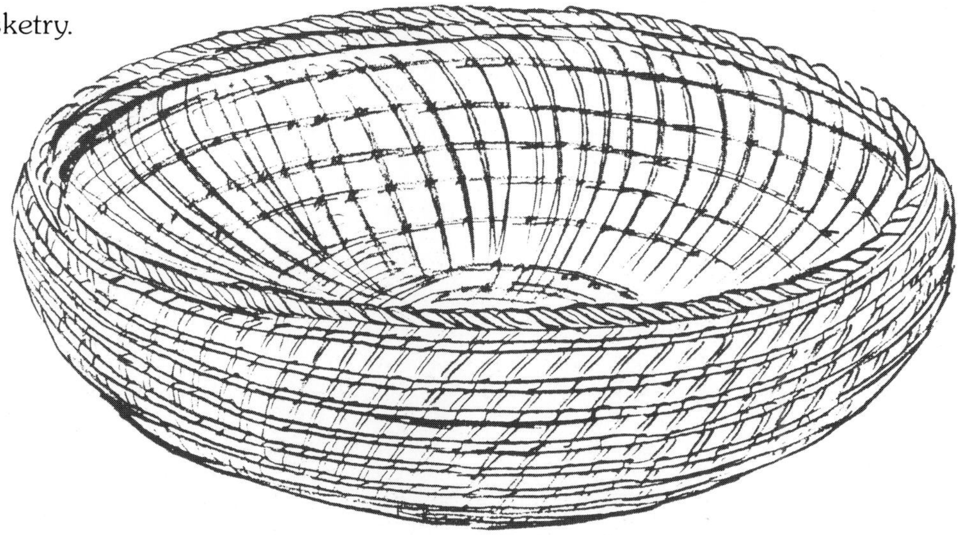

MATERIALS

1/8" (3 mm) #3 round reed
   30" (76 cm), 8 strands
   15" (38 cm), 16 strands
   14" (35.5 cm), 32 strands
   12" (30 cm), 32 strands
   9" (23 cm), 16 strands
   8½" (22 cm), 16 strands
Soak for 10 minutes.

1/32" (1 mm) #0 round reed
   10' (3 m), 30 strands
   Moisten.

¼" (6 mm) × 27½" (70 cm) willow twigs, 10 twigs
   Soak thoroughly for 2 days.

FINISHED SIZE: H 4" (10 cm) × 11½" (29.3 cm)

EQUIPMENT

Flower arrangement shears
Measuring tape
Single-edged knife
Needle-nosed pliers
Awl

INSTRUCTIONS

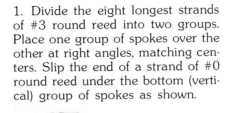

1. Divide the eight longest strands of #3 round reed into two groups. Place one group of spokes over the other at right angles, matching centers. Slip the end of a strand of #0 round reed under the bottom (vertical) group of spokes as shown.

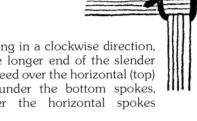

2. Working in a clockwise direction, bring the longer end of the slender twining reed over the horizontal (top) spokes, under the bottom spokes, and over the horizontal spokes again.

3. Repeat two times. Insert the end of another twining strand into the center of the top group of four spokes, dividing them in half.

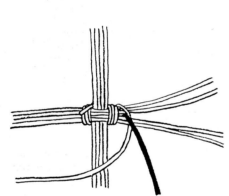

4. Pass the first twining strand over the first half of the spokes, under the second, and bring it to the front.

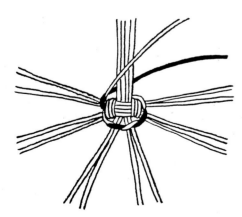

5. Divide the vertical group of spokes in half. Cross the twining strands so the first strand passes over and the inserted strand passes under the first half. Twine around the center, dividing the remaining groups of spokes in half as you go.

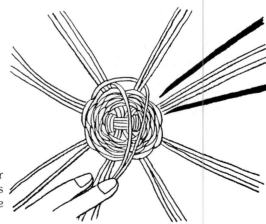

6. After twining for five rows, taper the ends of the 15" (38 cm) spokes and insert them on both sides of the radiating spokes.

7. Now you should have eight groups of four spokes (32 spokes). Split each group of four spokes in half and twine around the pairs for five rows.

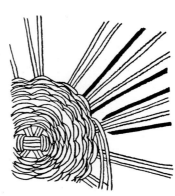

8. Taper the ends of the 14" (35.5 cm) spokes and insert them along both sides of the paired spokes for a total of 64 spokes. Twine around groups of four spokes for three rows.

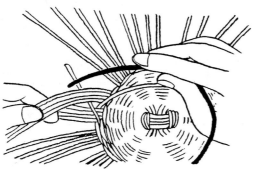

9. Join twining strands when necessary by inserting the end of a new strand behind a group of spokes. The next row of twining will secure the end.

10. Split the groups of four spokes into pairs and twine around the pairs for ten rows.

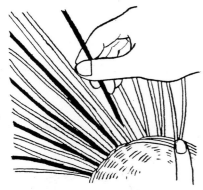

11. Taper the ends of the 12" (30 cm) spokes and insert them in the middle of each pair of spokes for a total of 96 spokes.

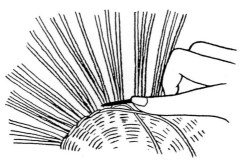

12. Sharpen the back of the thinner end of a willow twig and place it next to the previous row and on top of the radiating spokes. This additional element, called "ti," is always placed on the surface of the spokes.

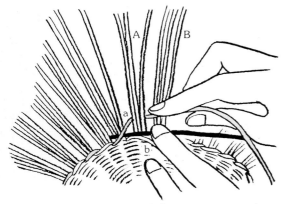

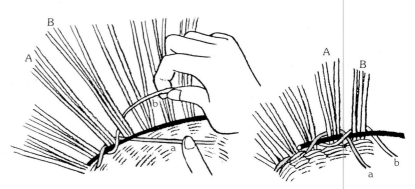

13. Pass the outer left twining strand **a** over the willow ti and the three spokes. Pass it under the next group of three spokes **A** and to the front from under the willow.

14. Pass the other twining strand **b** over the willow ti, under the reed spokes **B**, and to the front from under the willow ti.

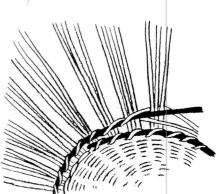

15. Keep the willow ti close to the previous row of twining.

16. When you near the beginning of the first row of willow ti, gradually slope your work upward to leave ¼" (6 mm) between the first and second rows.

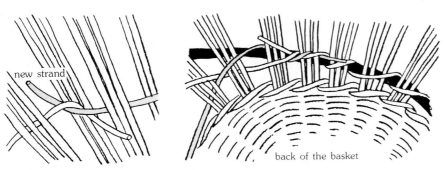

17. When joining twining strands in openwork the ends should be secured. Tie the ends together and twist them around each other.

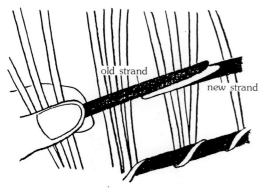

18. To add a new strand of willow ti, cut the back side of the old willow ti and the top side of the new one off at an angle. Slip the end of the new willow ti under the old. Twine over the joint in the normal way.

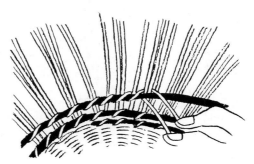

19. After finishing the second row, split each group of three spokes into pairs and single spokes. Ti-twine another row.

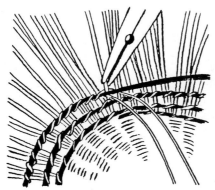

20. To start the sides of the basket, moisten the spokes, especially right above the last row of ti-twining. Squeeze this part of the spokes with needle-nosed pliers so the spokes do not snap when they are bent up.

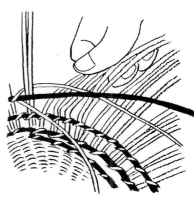

21. Hold the basket bottom vertically with the loose ends of the twining strands on top. Bend the spokes away from you.

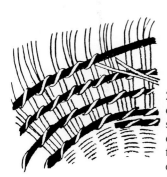

22. With the basket on your lap, continue to ti-twine pairs and single spokes for one row. Push down on the spokes as you twine to create a gradually rounded corner.

23. Split the pairs of spokes, and twine for two rows, keeping all the spokes at right angles to the willow ti.

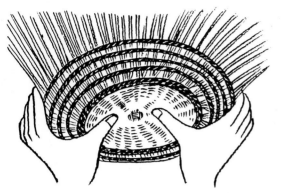

24. If the bottom of the basket begins to bulge outward, push it in, holding the whole basket in both hands as shown.

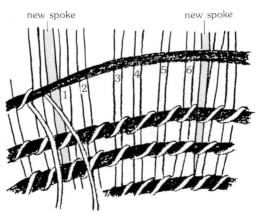

new spoke   new spoke

25. Insert one of the 9″ (23 cm) spokes after every six spokes. Push the end of each spoke down two rows. Twine one row.

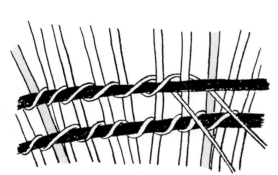

26. Split the pairs formed by the added spokes and twine one row.

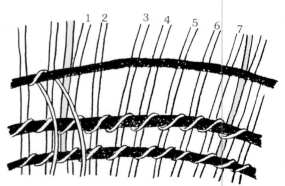

27. Insert one of the 8½″ (22 cm) spokes after every seventh spoke. Twine one row. Split the pairs and twine one row.

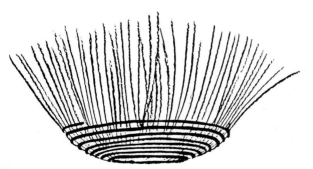

28. After the tenth row, the basket should be curved as shown.

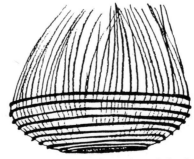

29. Begin to curve the sides of the basket in further as you twine another row. The basket should begin to curve like the illustration.

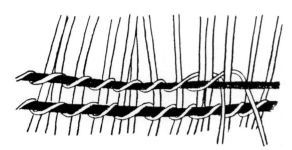

30. Twine a pair of spokes together, twine a single spoke, then another single spoke. Repeat this 2-1-1 pattern for rows twelve and thirteen.

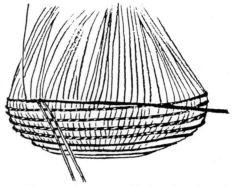

31. The spokes should be leaning in further.

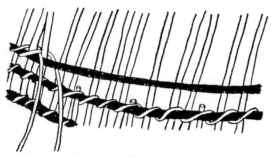

32. Cut off one of the spokes in each pair and twine another row (fourteenth).

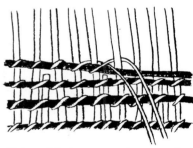

33. Twine this last row closer and closer to the previous row.

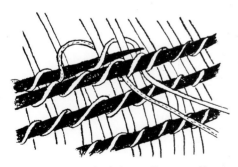

34. Cut the end of the willow ti off at an angle so the cut edge is against the previous row. To secure the ends of the twining strands, pass them through the previous row as shown and cut them off.

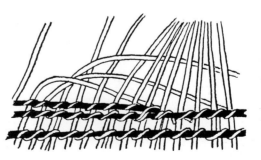

35. Moisten the spokes well. Bend each spoke over the next three spokes to the right and slip it in back of the fourth.

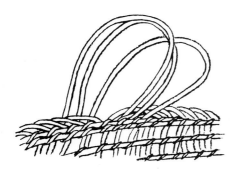

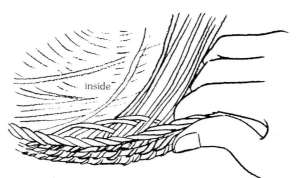

36. Bend all the spokes in the same manner. The last three spokes should be inserted under the three bent spokes at the beginning of the row.

37. Hold the basket so you are looking down directly over the edge. Bend each spoke over the next three spokes to the right and slip it in back of the fourth.

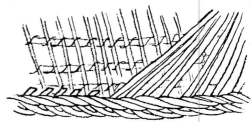

38. Bend and insert all the spokes in the same manner. Insert the last three spokes into the loops formed by the first three spokes in the row as shown.

39. To finish the basket, cut off all the ends of the spokes close under the border. Clip off the ends where you have joined strands and burn off any frayed reed (see Project 2, step 36).

4

COILED BASKET

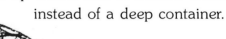

The colors and textures of willow twigs and the tips of white birch branches are combined and blended in this coiled basket. Besides being attractive, combining materials is a practical solution when one material runs out. Another solution is to stop coiling. In this technique, you are working on the border of the basket so you can stop any time although you might end up with a mat or shallow basket instead of a deep container.

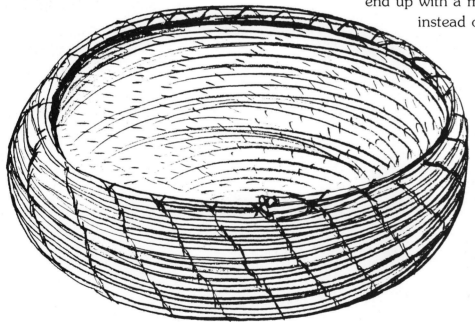

MATERIALS

1/32" (1 mm) willow twigs, 10 oz (300 gm) (when combined with birch branches)
Soak for 2 days.
  SUBSTITUTES: 1/32" (1 mm) #0 round reed (for both willow and birch)

1/16" (2 mm) dark red tips of white birch branches, 10 oz (300 gm) (when combined with willow twigs)
Soak for 2 days.

1 oz (30 gm) waxed hemp thread

FINISHED SIZE: H 4" (10 cm) × D 11" (28 cm)

EQUIPMENT

Measuring tape
Embroidery scissors
Single-edged or Swiss army knife
Flower arrangement shears
Blunt yarn needle

INSTRUCTIONS

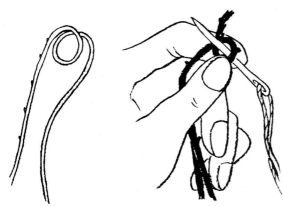

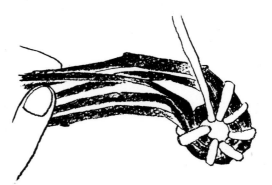

1. Make a small loop in the middle of three willow twigs. Insert a needle threaded as shown. Conceal the end of the thread by placing it between the willow twigs.

2. Holding the loose ends in your left hand, begin binding by wrapping the thread around the twigs from the inside of the loop out. To form the first row, work around the loop counterclockwise, binding with the thread six times. All work will be counterclockwise until the beginning of the curve of the basket wall in step 10.

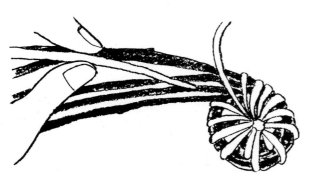

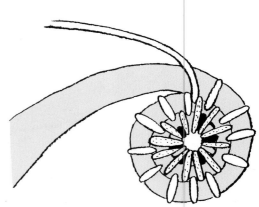

3. For the second row, coil the willow around the center circle. Fasten the willow to the first row by stitching from the center out and around the willow twelve times. This process of binding and coiling is what is usually termed coiling. Add tapered twigs to make a thicker bunch as necessary.

4. For the third row, wrap the twigs around again. Insert the needle into the bunch of willow that forms the previous row and to the left of the stitches made in the previous row. Wrap the thread around, making twelve stitches.

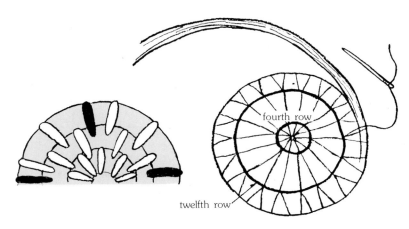

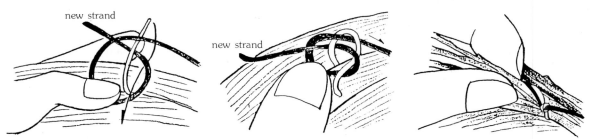

5. In the fourth row, increase six stitches for a total of 18. To increase, add a stitch between every other stitch in the third row. Coil rows five through eleven without increasing (see step 4). In the twelfth row, double the number of stitches to make 36 by making two stitches in a V-shape before each stitch in the eleventh row. Keep coiling until the work measures 3½″ (9 cm) in diameter. This forms the bottom of the basket.

6. When the binding thread runs out, join a new strand by making a tight knot. Slip the end of the strand to be joined over the old one, wrap it counterclockwise and slip it under the old strand and over itself as shown. Pass the end of the old strand over the new thread and through the loop formed in the previous step. Pull the ends to tighten the knot. Conceal the loose ends under the bunch of twigs to be coiled.

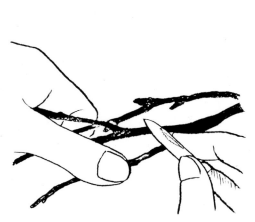

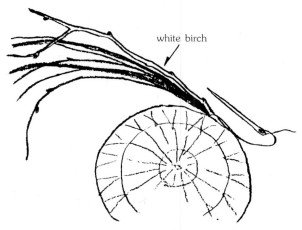

7. Prepare the white birch branches. To bring out the red shiny color of the bark, scrape the graying rust from the surface with the dull edge of a knife.

8. Add a branch of white birch by tapering the butt end and insert it in the outer edge of the bunch.

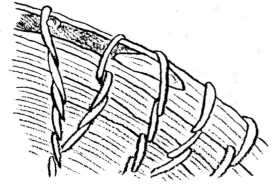

9. If the butt end is cut diagonally, the white core can be turned so it shows and provides color contrast.

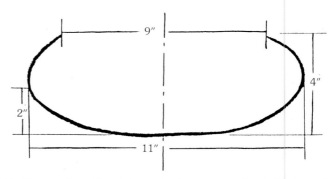

10. Shape the sides into a shallow curve. Push the bunch of branches up with your fingers, hold it in the desired position, and secure with the wrapping thread. For better control of the shaping, work with the inside of the basket toward you. You will now be coiling clockwise. Continue coiling until the work is 2″ (5 cm) deep and 11″ (28 cm) in diameter. Make the wall of the basket vertical by forming the next coil almost directly on top of the previous row. After a few rows, begin to curve the wall in again. The illustration shows the profile of the basket and its dimensions.

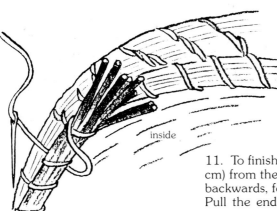

inside

11. To finish the basket, clip off the bunch of branches 1″ (2.5 cm) from the last stitch. Using the binding thread, stitch a row backwards, forming an X-pattern over the last row of stitches. Pull the end of the thread into the bunch and cut it off.

5

PLAITED BASKET

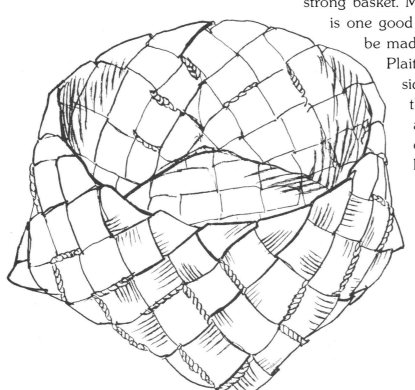

Some materials may have a very beautiful surface but a very rough underside. Some materials may be too thin or soft to make a strong basket. Making a double-layered basket is one good solution. Plaited baskets can be made double easily and attractively Plait a basket with the smooth side of the material inside, turn the strips over to the outside at the edge of the basket, and continue plaiting the outer layer over the inner basket.

MATERIALS

1¼″ (3.2 cm) × 3′ 4″ (1 m) banana sheaths, 16 strips
  Wet the sheaths, wrap them in a damp towel, and place in a plastic bag for about 1 hour.

8′ (2.4 m) × ¼″ (6 mm) ramie twine
  See Project 10, page 60.
  Estimate the necessary amount by weighing the bunch you start with, twine it, and measure the length.

FINISHED SIZE: H 4½″ (11.5 cm) × D 9″ (23 cm)

EQUIPMENT

Measuring tape
Awl
Felt marker
Clothespins
String
Atomizer

INSTRUCTIONS

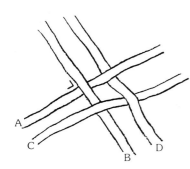

1. With the shiny side of the strips up, position strip **A** diagonally as shown. Cross strip **B** over **A** at a right angle. With **C** parallel to and below **A**, slip it over **B**. Weave **D** over **C** and under **A**. Slide the strips close to each other. This under-one/over-one process is called "plaiting."

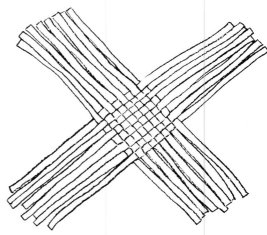

2. Continue plaiting all 16 strips in this under-one/over-one pattern until the center forms a 6¼" (16 cm) square.

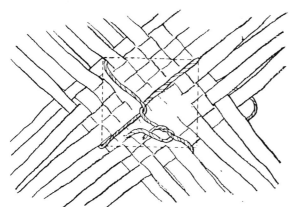

3. To keep the work tight as you bend the sides of the basket up, secure the plaited bottom with string. The string should pass through the midpoint of each side as shown. (This string can be removed after the corners have been plaited.)

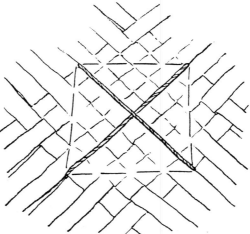

4. Turn your work over. Make lines connecting the four points formed by the string. This is the base of the basket. Use these four lines as fold lines when bending up the sides of the basket.

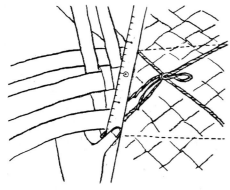

5. Turn the whole thing over again so that the shiny side faces up. Place a ruler along the fold line and fold up over it.

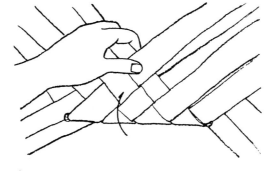

6. Fold up all four sides. At each corner of the basket one set of four strips will stick out to the right and another set to the left. These eight strips will be plaited one after the other in an under-one/over-one pattern.

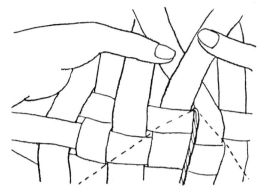

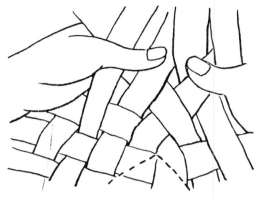

7. Take one set of four strips in your left hand and the other in your right hand and try to bring the two sets closer so they cross over each other. Start plaiting at the corner with the lowest two strips.

8. Plait the lowest strip in your right hand in an under-one/over-one pattern through the four strips in your left hand. Then plait the lowest strip in your left hand under-one/over-one through the four strips in your right hand.

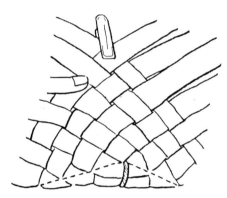

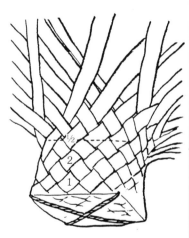

9. Plait all the strips in this under-one/over-one pattern.

10. Plait the strips at the other three corners. Plait the strips upward until you can see three diamonds in a vertical line up the side of the basket. Mark a horizontal line through the middle of the third diamond at the top of the basket. This will be the basket edge. Mark all the way around the basket.

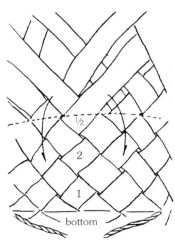

11. Fold the pair of strips forming the third diamond to the outside along the horizontal line. This is the start of the outer layer.

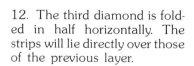

12. The third diamond is folded in half horizontally. The strips will lie directly over those of the previous layer.

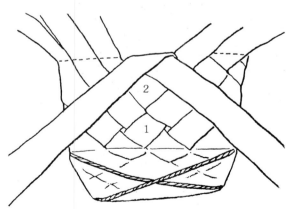

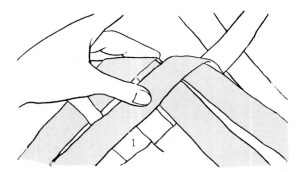

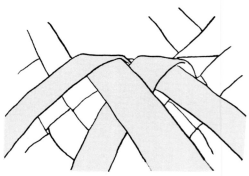

13. Fold down the next pair of strips to the right in the same way.

14. To maintain the under-one/over-one pattern on the outer layer, slip the left strip of the second pair under the right strip of the first pair.

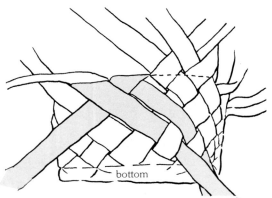

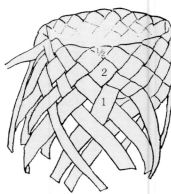

15. Each strip in the outer layer is placed directly over the strip of the inner layer in the same position. To keep the strips in place, pass them under the strips of the inner layer once in a while.

16. Plait the outer layer so that its under-one/over-one pattern corresponds exactly with that of the inner layer. Plait until you can see two and a half vertical diamonds in the outer layer. Turn the basket upside down.

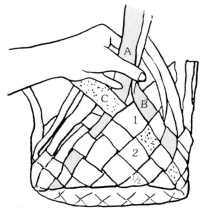

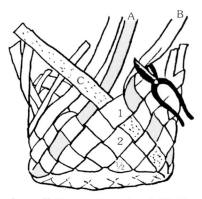

17. Find the corner. Two strips (**A** and **B**) should meet above the corner diamond. Begin plaiting the bottom of the basket.

18. Cut off **B** to a length of 2″ (5 cm).

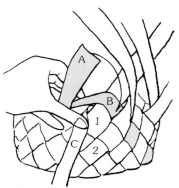

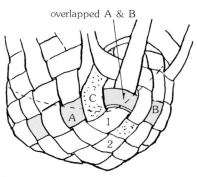

overlapped A & B

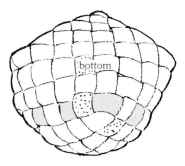

bottom

19. Slip **B** under **A**, bending **B** around the corner. Fold **A** over **B** and tuck its end under the plaiting. **A** will lie directly over **B**.

20. Bend **C** over the overlapped **A** and **B**. Plait **C** with the strip on the left, then with the strip on the right. These newly plaited strips will overlap each other like **A** and **B**.

21. Continue plaiting at each corner until all 32 ends of the 16 strips are joined, cut off, and plaited with each other. This finishes the outer layer.

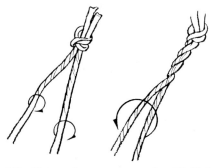

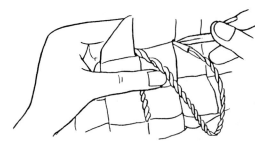

23. Use an awl to open spaces between strips in the basket, thread the twine through, and stitch the layers together. Any pattern of stitching may be used.

22. Using the ramie, make 8' (2.4 m) of ¼" (6 mm) twine. Divide the ramie into two bunches. Tie the ends and pin the knot down. Twist each bunch clockwise, then twist the two bunches together counterclockwise. Add new fibers as necessary (see Project 10).

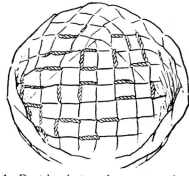

24. Besides being decorative, these twine stitches reinforce the structure by holding the two layers together more tightly.

Woven basket, Project 2, page 17; Twined openwork basket, Project 3, page 25; Coiled basket, Project 4, page 33; Plaited basket, Project 5, page 37.

The Properties and Preparation of Materials

When students at workshops ask me, "Can I use this?" or "How should I prepare this?", I pause, afraid of sounding rude or frivolous, and then reply, "However you like." To me, this is the kindest answer that is at the same time faithful to the rich potential of the material. So, I always modify my answer by adding, "That is, it mostly depends on what you intend to make."

If you have read the first part of this section explaining the interplay between form, material, and method, you will understand my answer. And you will also understand that the directions for preparing any given material can be applied to a wide range of similar materials.

In my experience, traditional know-how and techniques are so varied and numerous that within them the basketmaker can find justification for almost any technique or method he decides to use. That is, nothing is wrong, and conversely, nothing is right. Therefore, there is no need to worry about using and preparing materials the "right" way. The basketmaker must be his own judge and discover the best way to prepare and use materials for each basket through his own efforts and experience.

To give you some basis from which to judge, I have extracted information on the properties and preparation of materials from various basket traditions and generalized them rather than presenting an overview of the traditions themselves. Although this generalization is mine, I feel it can be applied to the basketmaking of others. Based on my study of and experiments with my native tradition and others, including those of the American Indians, I have translated traditional methods of preparation that were too specialized or developed to fit a particular niche into more universal terms.

The five projects that follow will help you prepare materials used in other projects in this book without worrying about the "right" way. And once you rid yourself of the idea that you must have the same tools as those used by professional basketmakers in other countries and cultures, you will find that the common tools around you will work quite well. In Tools, page 141, I have listed and described the tools that I use every day with some suggestions for substitutions.

WHAT MATERIALS CAN WE USE?

Baskets can be made from any fibrous material as long as it is flexible and not too short. Even metals can be used if prepared in fibrous forms such as thread or thin foil. Our ancestors seem to have used whatever was available and workable. Historically, trees and plants have been the most common source of basket materials. Plants that through the test of time have been identified as excellent sources of fiber are called "fiber plants." This book concentrates on plant materials.

WHAT PART OF THE PLANT CAN WE USE?

Different parts of plants yield fibrous materials in a variety of shapes and forms.

FROND. LEAF: narrow, long, flat material (when used whole), extracted filaments

STEM. STALK: long, slender material (when used whole), inner bark fiber (bast fiber)

TREE BARK: long strips or sheets of outer bark and inner bark (bast layer)

WOOD. STALK: long ribbonlike material (splint)

TWIG. YOUNG SHOOT: rodlike material (when used whole), split

VINE. RUNNER: very long, pliable round material (when used whole), split (A thick vine also yields inner bark and woody core.)

ROOT: very flexible, round material (when used whole), split

FRUIT: soft, cottonlike, loose fiber

HOW CAN WE FIND THE USEFUL PROPERTIES OF PLANTS?

When you want to use plants that are unfamiliar to you, try to determine their properties before collecting them in any quantity. The best way to familiarize yourself with various plants is to experiment with each one and check its properties in plant and tree books and magazines. The following are some general tests.

To test the flexibility and strength of a frond or stem; bend, twist, and pull it, both when it is fresh and when it is withered (not dried). Sometimes beating the coarse fiber of the strand will soften it and make it more flexible (see Project 22). To test a shoot, vine, or root, bend it into a loop, both when whole and split.

To test whether you can make a split (or splint) out of a vine, stalk, or tree, split it (or make splints) while it is fresh (see Projects 8 and 9).

To test the strength of the bast layer of a tree or vine, or the stem of a dicotyledon, peel it while it is fresh to see if it will come off in one long piece.

HOW CAN WE USE MATERIALS?

To prepare most materials, air dry in the shade after collecting, store until they reach a stable condition, and just before using, soak in water until pliable enough to work with. Some plants can be used whole; others require simple processing such as removing unusable parts or more elaborate processing to transform them into a useable form. Sometimes materials are dyed, painted, or polished to preserve and decorate them.

The proper time to collect materials can vary according to how they will be used. Traditionally, craftsmen determined the best time for each material very strictly according to its intended function. However, our purpose in making baskets differs from theirs, and naturally the best time to collect materials will also differ. And unfortunately, contemporary basketmakers cannot always choose when they collect materials. So it is important to know how the properties of plants differ depending on the seasons and conditions they are collected in and learn to use these properties. The following information will give you some idea of how these properties vary according to season and growing conditions.

While the plant is growing or is producing fruit, from early spring through summer, it contains a nourishing sap which bagworms and mildew love.

During the active growth season, the outer bark can be removed easily.

The fiber of an annual plant matures at its seeding time.

A plant cut in its inactive season has a dense inner structure.

A plant cut while it is receiving ample sunshine will turn blacker later.

Plants that receive plenty of water, sun, and nourishment as they grow are large, rough textured, porous, and more flexible.

Plants that are in the shade and receive a limited amount of water grow slower and are small, dense, and stiffer.

Thoughtful collecting requires that you keep an eye on the future. You can help nature without harming it by trimming young shoots such as willow and hibiscus yearly to encourage growth, or removing objects from the path of vines like akebia to produce straight runners. But nature should never be destroyed. In order to insure a continuing source of materials, plants should not be uprooted. *Whatever you do, do not steal plants from their owners or from nature to make your baskets.*

Immediately after the material is collected, it should be sorted according to its size, thickness, length, and prospective use (rod, split/splint, bark, etc.). Lay out flat sheets of materials like cherry bark; make bundles of fronds, rods, branches, twigs, and dwarf bamboo leaves; coil vines and the bark of trees inside out if the bark is flexible and long enough; and leave logs and saplings as they are.

Some material may require preliminary processing before storage. Any dirt or stains should be removed right away. The outer bark can be removed most easily when the material is fresh. If you think you might remove the bark of a rather large vine or branch later (after it has dried), split it in half before storing so that when it is soaked it will absorb water much faster. Vines collected in the early spring through summer should be boiled immediately to kill any bagworms inside.

Some processing can wait until the basket design is determined. To soften coarse fiber such as rice, sedge, grass, or wheat so it can be bent, moisten the fiber by spraying it with or dipping it in water, then beat the fiber on a wooden base with a wooden mallet. Bark can be removed in several ways. If the bark is useable and soft like that of mulberry or vines, carefully peel it off; if it is unuseable and on a rodlike material such as willow, pull it through a metal hole; and if it is unuseable and thick and crumbly like the bark on a walnut or cedar log or large wisteria vine, scrape it off with the blade of a knife, then carefully remove the useable inner bark. To extract a large quantity of sturdy filaments out of the thick, meaty leaves or stems of plants like the Japanese kudzu, Indian jute, or Central American century plant, soak them in warm water or boil them, depending on how warm the season and your climate are. Keep them covered and between 25° and 40°. Wash or scrape the rotten fleshy part away. Small quantities of filaments can be removed with a knife.

The properties of some materials can be changed to suit the method and structure. Weak, slender materials like cattails or rush can be made stronger and larger by braiding or bundling several strands (see Project 10). Strong, large materials like maple logs can be reduced if they are shredded or split along the grain (see Project 9). Brown ash and large wisteria vines can be separated into splints along the growth rings by beating the whole log or vine.

Some extra touches can improve the appearance and quality of the material. Cherry bark can be scraped and sanded to bring out the color (see Project 7). Vegetable dyes can provide color variation (see Project 11). Apply *urushi* lacquer, water-resistant persimmon juice (commercially available as *kaki shibu*), or dyeing extract to a finished basket with a brush or wiping cloth, or simply pour the liquid over the basket. Camellia oil and pure vegetable wax preserve the shine of materials. To line a basket with *washi* (Japanese handmade paper made of long natural fibers), use a mixture of egg white and rice starch as an adhesive. Boil rice in a small amount of water until it is sticky and pasty, cool, and add egg white.

cattails   long, narrow fronds

bamboo   slender stalks

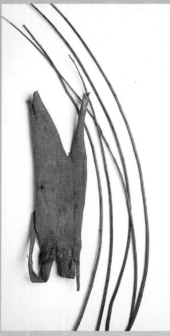

willow   shoots and bark

paper mulberry   bark

maple

splints

ramie

bast fiber

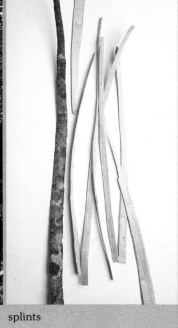

wisteria

vine and bark

akebia

vine

sinomenine

vine

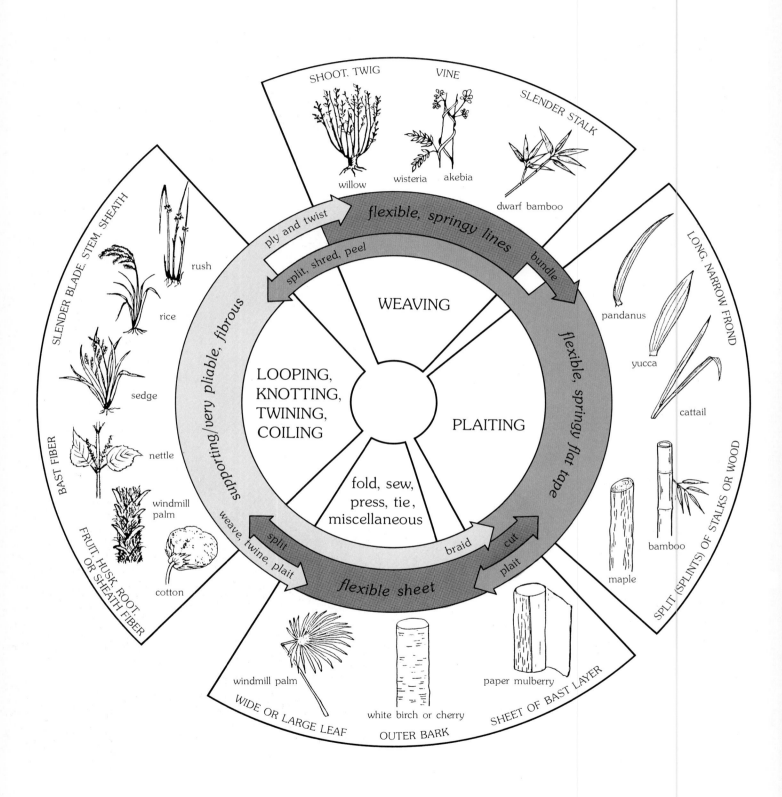

This pictorial chart shows typical combinations of plant materials with construction methods. Read this chart from the center out when you want to know what type of plants you should collect for a certain method and from the outside in to find suitable techniques for a certain type of plant. The arrows indicate how to transform materials in one section into new forms that will have properties equivalent to the materials in another section. The lists of fiber plants in each section give the genus and English and Japanese names of plants in each genus. Those in parenthesis are close equivalents although not necessarily materials used in basketry.

SHOOT, TWIG

Salix sp.	willow, *koriyanagi*
Hibiscus sp.	hibiscus, hau, *ohamabo*
Hamamelis sp.	witch hazel, *mansaku*
Acacia sp.	acacia
Cercis sp.	redbud, *(hanazuo)*
Corylus sp.	American hazel
Rhus sp.	sumac, *(urushi, haze)*
Olea sp.	olive
Coronus sp.	dogwood, *(mizuki)*
Berchemia sp.	(supple jack), *kumayanagi*

VINE

Akebia sp.	akebia
Sinomenium sp.	sinomenine, *tsuzurafuji*
Wisteria sp.	wisteria, *fuji*
Pueraria sp.	kudzu, *kuzu*
Vitis sp.	grape, *yamabudo*
Actinidia sp.	silvervine, *nikyo, sarunashi, matatabi*
Lonicera sp.	honeysuckle, *suikazura*

SLENDER STALK

Calamus sp.	rattan (round reed), to
Daemonorops sp.	rattan (round reed), to
Sasa sp.	dwarf bamboo, *kumazasa*

LONG, NARROW FROND

Cocos sp.	coconut palm, *koko-yashi*
Musa sp.	abaca, banana, *itobasho*
Pandanus sp.	pandanus, hala, screw pine, *takonoki*
Yucca sp.	yucca, *kimigayoran*
Sansevieria sp.	sansevieria, bowstring hemp
Agave sp.	agave, century plant, henequen, *ryuzetsuran*
Typha sp.	cattail, *gama*
Phormium sp.	New Zealand flax, *maoran*
Dracaena sp.	dracaena
Ananas sp.	pineapple

SPLITS (SPLINTS) OF STALKS OR WOOD

Phyllostachys sp.	bamboo, *madake, mosodake*
Pleioblastus sp.	bamboo, *shinodake, medake*
Arundinaria sp.	carrizo, swamp cane, river cane
Actinidia sp.	silvervine, *matatabi, nikyo*
Acer sp.	maple, *itayakaede*
Rhus sp.	sumac, *yamaurushi*
Quercus sp.	white oak, *mizunara*
Fraximus sp.	ash *(toneriko)*
Salix sp.	willow, *koriyanagi*
Ulmus sp.	elm, *(nire)*
Chamaecyparis sp.	(white cedar), *hinoki*
Cryptomeria sp.	cryptomeria, *sugi*
Taxus sp.	yew, *ichi-i*

SHEET OF BAST LAYER

Cryptomeria sp.	cryptomeria, *sugi*
Chamaecyparis sp.	(white cedar), *hinoki*
Juglans sp.	walnut, *kurumi*
Carya sp.	hickory
Populus sp.	poplar
Ulmus sp.	elm, *ohyo*
Juniperus sp.	red cedar, *(nezu)*
Thuja sp.	Western red cedar, *(kurobe)*
Tilia sp.	basswood, linden, *shinanoki*
Adansonia sp.	baobab
Touchardia sp.	olona
Broussonetia sp.	paper mulberry, *kajinoki, kozo*
Morus sp.	mulberry, *kuwa*
Ficus sp.	wild fig
Hibiscus sp.	hibiscus, hau, *ohamabo*

OUTER BARK

Prunus sp.	cherry, *yamazakura*
Betula sp.	white birch, *shirakaba*

WIDE OR LARGE LEAF

Trachycarpus sp.	windmill palm, *shuro*
Livistona sp.	livistona, *kuba*
Sasa sp.	dwarf bamboo, *kumazasa*

FRUIT, HUSK, ROOT, OR SHEATH FIBER

Trachycarpus sp.	windmill palm, *shuro*

Picea sp.	Sitka spruce, *(momi)*
Freycinetia sp.	freycinetia, *tsuru-adan, kasokaso*
Chamaecyparis sp.	(white cedar), *hinoki*
Martynia sp.	unicorn plant, *(tsunogoma)*
Zea sp.	corn
Gossypium sp.	cotton, *wata*
Cocos sp.	coconut palm
Ceiba sp.	kapok

BAST FIBER

Apocynum sp.	Indian hemp, *bashikurumon*
Hibiscus sp.	hibiscus, hau, *ohamabo*
Corchorus sp.	jute, *tsuna-so*
Laportea sp.	(wood nettle), *aiko*
Urtica sp.	nettle, *irakusa*
Boehmeria sp.	ramie, *choma, karamushi*

SLENDER BLADE, STEM, SHEATH

Carex sp.	sedge, *kansuge*
Scirpus sp.	tule, *futo-i*
Lepironia sp.	ampela
Cyperus sp.	cyperus, *kanso, kaengayatsuri, shichito-i*
Juncus sp.	soft rush, *igusa*
Imperata sp.	(cogon), *chigaya*
Elymus sp.	(wild rye), *hama-ninniku, tenki-so*
Poa sp.	snow grass, *(ichigotsunagi)*
Sporobolus sp.	tussock grass, dropseed, *(nezumi-no-o)*
Hierochloe sp.	sweet grass, *(kobo)*
Stipa sp.	esparto
Deschampsia sp.	hair grass, *(komesusuki)*
Secale sp.	rye
Triticum sp.	wheat, *komugi*
Hordeum sp.	barley, *omugi*
Oryza sp.	rice, *ine*
Iris sp.	iris, *(ayame)*
Hemerocallis sp.	daylily, *(kanzo)*
Zingiber sp.	ginger, *shoga, myoga*
Raphia sp.	raffia

HOW TO PREPARE PAPER MULBERRY BARK

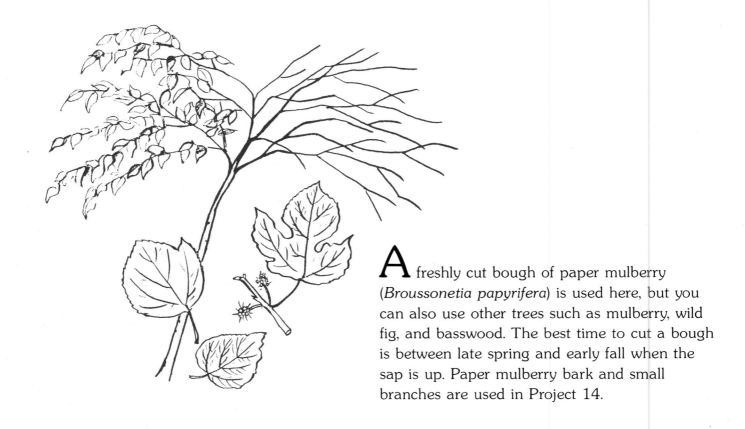

A freshly cut bough of paper mulberry (*Broussonetia papyrifera*) is used here, but you can also use other trees such as mulberry, wild fig, and basswood. The best time to cut a bough is between late spring and early fall when the sap is up. Paper mulberry bark and small branches are used in Project 14.

MATERIALS
2⅜″ (6 cm) × 9′ (2.7 m) freshly cut bough from a paper mulberry tree

AFTER PREPARATION:
 From the main bough
  1½″ (4 cm) × 8′ (2.4 m)
  6¾″ (17 cm) × 8′ (2.4 m)
 From the larger branches
  ¾″ (2 cm) × 9′ (2.7 m)

EQUIPMENT
Single-edged knife

INSTRUCTIONS

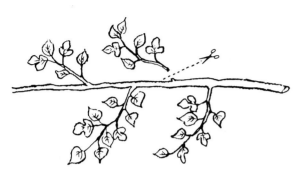

1. Cut the branches off the bough and set them aside.

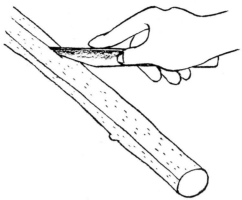

2. With the knife, make two parallel cuts about 1½″ (4 cm) apart down the length of the bough.

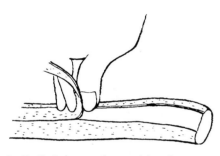

3. Pull the strip formed by the cuts upward. The strip consists of both the outer bark and the inner bast layer.

4. Roll up the strip with its bark side in to prevent the sides from curling under when the strip dries.

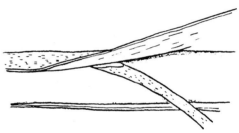

5. Cut the end off a small twig at an angle. Use the pointed end of this twig to lift and loosen the rest of the bark.

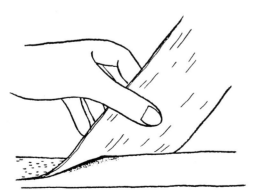

6. Starting at the bottom, carefully remove the bark from the bough. Roll it up with its bark side in.

7. To remove the bark from the larger branches, make a single slit down the length of the branches. Repeat steps 5 and 6. The smaller branches can also be used as loops or handles and should not be discarded (see Project 14). Bend them in half, fasten with string, and let them dry.

7

HOW TO PREPARE
CHERRY BARK

A cherry tree, especially a mountain cherry, yields dark red strong outer bark with an enamel shine. Sometimes the bark is covered with a thin gray skin or a rather thick corky substance, but this can be scraped off with a knife. Prepare cherry bark from either a log cut when the sap is up or a dried sheet. Coiled baskets by American Indians in the Northwest Pacific use cherry bark tapes in a folded overlay technique called "imbrication." Cherry bark is used in Projects 2 and 14.

MATERIALS
4″ (10 cm) × 12″ (30 cm) cherry log
　The diameter of the log determines the length of the strips that can be made. Strips should be cut with the grain. In cherry trees and birches, the outer bark grain runs horizontally around the trunk, and the inner bark grain runs vertically. In cedar and many other trees, the grain of the outer and inner bark runs up and down the trunk.

AFTER PREPARATION:
12″ (30 cm) × 12″ (30 cm) sheet of cherry bark

EQUIPMENT
Bamboo split knife
Fine emery paper
Soft cloth
Camellia or olive oil
Clothespins (if using dried sheet)
Piece of heavy leather (if using dried sheet)

INSTRUCTIONS

1. Clean the cherry bark by scraping it with the knife. Hold the cutting edge of the knife at a right angle to the surface of the log. Pull the blade toward you while pushing down on the knife. Repeat until the entire surface has been cleaned.

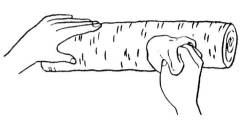

2. Rub the surface with very fine emery paper. Then polish the bark with a soft cloth moistened with camellia or olive oil.

3. To remove the bark from the log, cut a slit in the surface down the length of the log.

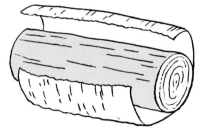

4. Using the tip of the knife, very carefully lift up the cut edges. Be careful to remove only the outer bark at this time.

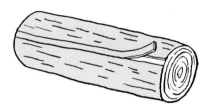

5. When the outer bark has been taken off, cut another slit down the length of the inner bark, parallel to the first cut. Pull off the narrow strip formed between the first and second slits. Then remove all of the inner bark.

6. Press the outer bark between layers of newspaper to flatten it. Let it dry. Dry the inner bark as it is.

To use dried sheets of cherry bark

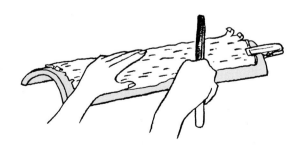

To use dried sheets of cherry bark, first soak them in water for about half a day. Pull the inner bark away from the outer bark with your hands. Use clothespins to fasten the outer bark with the grain lengthwise to a curved scraping base. Here a large bamboo stalk cut in half has been used. Protect your lap with a piece of leather and scrape with the grain to avoid ripping the bark. Clean and polish the bark as in steps 1 and 2 above.

8

HOW TO SPLIT BAMBOO STALKS

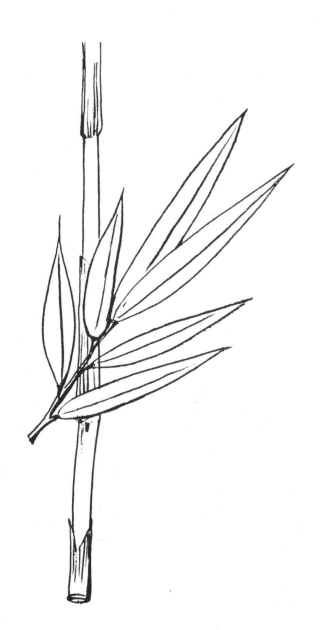

The bamboo used here is *shinodake*, a small type of bamboo belonging to the genus *Pleioblastus*. It has a slender hollow stalk less than ⅝″ (1.5 cm) in diameter and over 7′ (2 m) high. *Medake* and *madake* are also widely used in Japan. *Madake*, of the genus *Phyllostachys*, is a larger type of bamboo which sheds its sheaths in the growing season. It can be split in about the same way as the smaller types. You can also use river cane or carrizo, plants of the genus *Arundinaria*. Collect *shinodake* or other bamboo plants at the beginning of winter and store them whole or in coiled splits. Split bamboo stalks are used in Projects 14 and 18.

MATERIALS
⅝″ (1.5 cm) × 7′ (2 m) bamboo stalk

AFTER PREPARATION: After splitting until you have one split of the required size, estimate how many splits your skill will produce. Bamboo is not cut but split along the grain. The knife, mostly used as a wedge, is needed only to make the initial cut at the bottom and to cut through the joints.

EQUIPMENT
Bamboo split knife
Cloth
Pieces of leather

INSTRUCTIONS

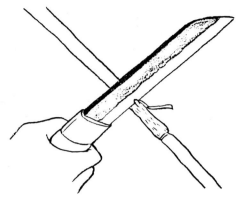

1. Remove the sheaths by scraping lightly with the edge of a knife.

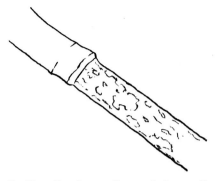

2. Usually the surface of the stalk is spotted with black stains.

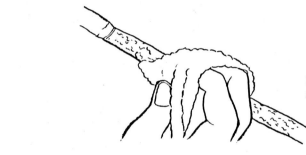

3. Wipe the stains off with a moistened coarse cloth.

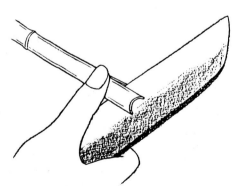

4. Use a knife to split the stalk in half from the bottom up. Protect your lap and your left hand with pieces of leather. Rest your right thumb and forefinger on opposite sides of the stalk just in front of the blade. This helps prevent the blade from suddenly hitting your left hand when the stalk splits further than expected.

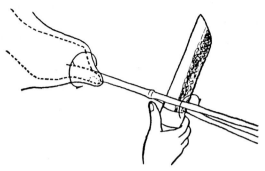

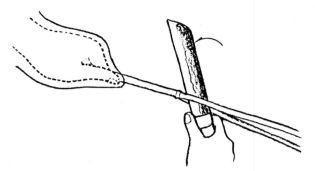

5. When you come to a joint, press the stalk against your right knee and try to twist the blade clockwise while you twist the stalk counterclockwise with your left hand.

6. Bending the blade toward the stalk as you twist will also make splitting easier.

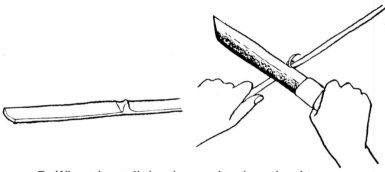

7. When the stalk has been split, place the shiny outside of the stalk on your knee, and lay the knife with its cutting edge at a slight angle of about 25° on the stalk. Pull the split toward you. Keep scraping off the inner part until the stalk is the required thickness.

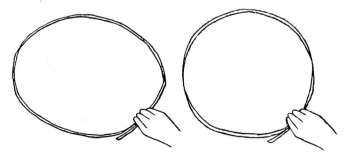

8. Make a circle with the split to see if it is even in thickness. If the split is not even, the circle will not be perfectly round as the thicker parts tend to stay straight. Scrape any parts that are too thick.

9. The edges of the split bamboo are sharp and should be dulled. Stand the split on its side and scrape the edge slightly. Adjust the width of the splits if necessary.

HOW TO SPLIT A MAPLE LOG

Maple is a shiny, smooth, white wood in which the growth rings are not very distinct. A fifteen-year-old sapling makes good splints. It should be straight and knotless for at least 26″ (66 cm). Maple should be cut in winter. Trees of the genus *Quercus* (white oak) or the genus *Rhus* (sumac) are traditionally used in a similar way. Make splints from ash (*Fraximus* sp.) by pounding the log with a mallet to separate the growth layers. The splints can be pulled off with your hands. Maple splints are used in Project 15.

MATERIALS
2½″ (6.5 cm) × 26″ (66 cm) maple log
   Soak for 2 to 3 days if using a dried log.

3 pieces of hardwood for making wedges

AFTER PREPARATION:
120 maple splints ¹⁄₁₆″ (2 mm) × 26″ (66 cm)
   After splitting the first eighth of the log into the required thickness, you can estimate the total number of splints. The number will vary according to your skill and the quality of the log.

EQUIPMENT
Bamboo split knife or small hatchet
Wooden mallet
Buck knife
Piece of leather

INSTRUCTIONS

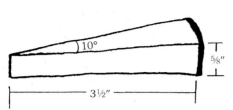

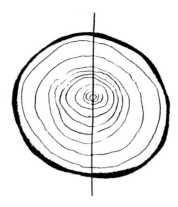

1. To make a wedge, whittle a small piece of hardwood into a 10° wedge about 3½" (9 cm) long and ⅝" (1.5 cm) high. Make two more wedges.

2. Mark the first split line through the center of the log on the butt end, using the center of the growth rings instead of the geometrical center of the log. (The sunny side of the tree trunk usually grows faster so these two centers will not be the same.)

3. Try to place the split lines so the log is divided into equally thick halves as this will make splitting easier. Use the mallet to drive the knife in at the split line. Insert two wedges into both sides of the opening and pound them deeper and downward with the mallet.

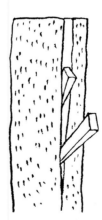

4. Remove the big knife, or hatchet, and continue to drive the wedges deeper and downward.

5. When the wedges cannot be driven any further, drive the third wedge in below the first until the first can be pulled out easily.

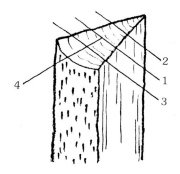

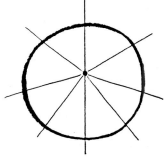

6. Then drive the freed wedge in below the wedge on the other side of the log. Repeat this process until the entire log has been split.

7. Divide the halves into quarters by splitting them in half, being careful to cut through the center of the growth rings and not the geometrical center. Cut each of the quarters in half, again cutting through the center of the growth rings.

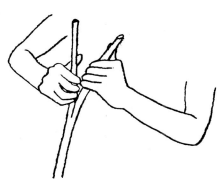

8. Split each of the eight pieces along their growth layers with your hands, first at line 1, then at 2 and 3. Then cut the outermost flat piece in half across its width at line 4.

9. Repeat until the desired thickness and width are .reached. To split straight, try to pull equally on each side and to bend the splints evenly. If one side is bent down more than the other, it will tend to become thinner and thinner until it tapers off at the end.

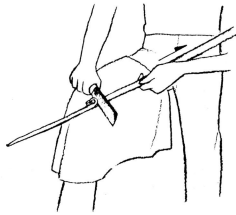

10. Scrape the splints with a knife. Protect your lap with a piece of leather. Set the maple splint on your lap and lay the knife with the cutting edge at a slight angle on the splint. Pull the splint toward you (see Project 8).

HOW TO MAKE TWINE AND BRAID

Making tightly-twined cordage is an important and useful basic technique in folk art basketry. Two methods are shown here: one for stronger grass stems, the other for very soft, fine, threadlike plant fibers. Rushes of the genus *Juncus* grow in swamps and have slender cylindrical stems with a spongy white inner pith. The type used here, *Juncus effusus*, has a cluster of brown seeds slightly above the middle of the stem. This is the type of rush used for the surface of tatami mats. Any strong rushes or sedges work well for twine. The second method can be used with ramie or jute. Soft rush twine is used in Projects 19 and 20, and the ramie twine is used in Project 5.

Braiding is another important technique. The instructions are for a six-strand braid made of cattail, a plant of the genus *Typha*, which grows in marshes. It has straight long blades and a stem with a brown spike on top. Collect cattails in the early fall after the spike has matured. Dry them straight in the sun. Also suitable for braiding are strong blades with parallel veins such as irises or daylilies; sheaths of ginger; whole stems or leaves of rushes, grasses, and sedges; and the bast fiber of trees. A six-strand cattail braid is used in Project 15.

Soft rush twine

MATERIALS

4 stems of soft rush to start with (an even number works best)
Twine the initial group of stems together, measure the length, and estimate how many stems you will need for the required length.

Moisten. (If stiffer grass or sedge stems such as rice straw are used, beat the moistened stems with a wooden mallet to soften them.)

AFTER PREPARATION: Prepare the twine to the required length using the information above.

EQUIPMENT

Clothespin
String

INSTRUCTIONS

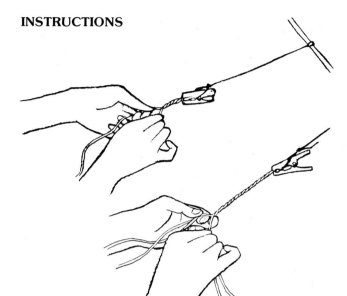

1. Begin with four or more rush stems. Divide them in half and tie the ends of the two groups together. To make the twine easier to start, fasten a clothespin to a stationary object, and clip it on the knot. Twist each group of premoistened stems counterclockwise and twist the groups together clockwise. Continue until you have at least one foot of twine.

2. Remove the starting knot from the clothespin and sit on it to secure it, with the twine on your right.

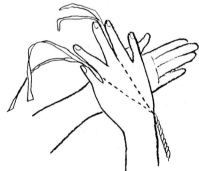

3. Pick up one group of stems (here two strands) between the thumb and index finger of your right hand. Continue to hold the group as you place it on the palm of your left hand near your wrist. The other group of stems should be lying across the middle of your left palm, the loose ends near your fingers.

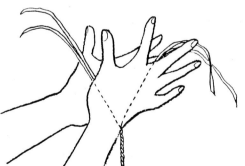

4. Slide your right hand over your left palm, pressing down and turning your hand at the same time. This rolling motion twists each group of stems as well as twisting them together.

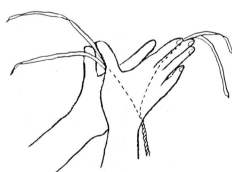

5. Notice how the hands start out almost at right angles to each other and end up pointing in the same direction.

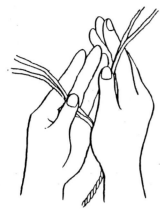

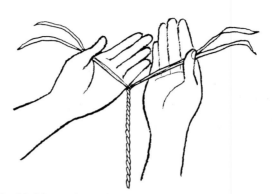

6. When the two groups reach the finger-tips of your left hand and get too close together to continue, catch the right group between the index finger and thumb of your right hand.

7. Holding the other group under your left thumb, open your hand as shown.

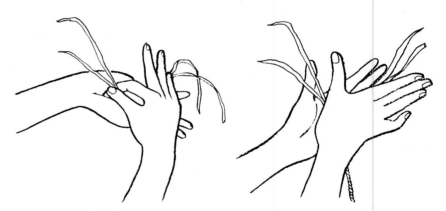

8. Place your hands as in step 3 and repeat steps 4 through 7.

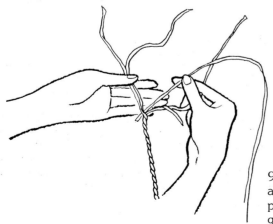

9. To join a new stem, hold the groups apart with your fingers and open your palms. Slip the new strand under the left group and continue making twine.

Very soft fiber twine

MATERIALS

Bundle of ramie. Depending on the desired thickness, use anywhere from 2 filaments to 2 bunches.
  Weigh and make twine with the bunch that you start with, measure the length, and estimate how much you will need for the required length.

AFTER PREPARATION: Prepare the twine to the required length using the information above.

EQUIPMENT

24″ (61 cm) of string
Bowl of water

2. With the bunch attached to the knob, stand in front of the door, and hold the bunch to your left. Place the bowl of water on a chair or table within reach.

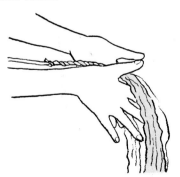

5. Slide your right hand toward your left fingertips, rolling the two bunches between both palms.

INSTRUCTIONS

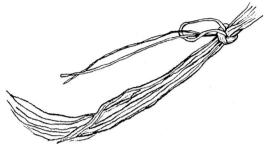

1. Make a bunch with the loose fiber, knot one end and attach a 24″ (61 cm) piece of string. Tie the string to a doorknob.

3. Divide the bunch in half and moisten your palms.

6. When the two bunches get too close to continue, hold the left bunch between the thumb and index finger of your left hand and hold the right bunch between the thumb and index finger of your other hand. Flip the right bunch across the left bunch quickly so that the ends of the fibers do not become entangled.

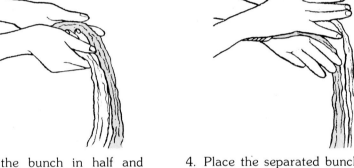

4. Place the separated bunches on your left palm, one over your wrist and one over your thumb. Press your right palm over the bunches.

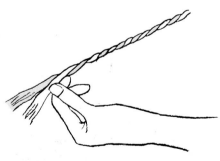

7. Place the bunches in the same position as step 4, and repeat steps 5 and 6. New strands of fiber can be joined in the same way as for rush stems (see step 9 of the instructions for soft rush twine).

Six-strand braid

MATERIALS
Strands of dried cattail (in multiples of six)
  Braid the first six strands, measure the length, and estimate
  how many cattails you will need for the required length.
  Soak for 15 minutes and keep wrapped in a plastic sheet
  for more than 1 hour before using.

AFTER PREPARATION: Braid to the required length using the information above.

EQUIPMENT
String

INSTRUCTIONS

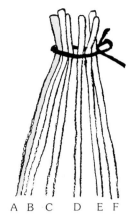

1. Tie the ends of six strands together with string.

A B C D E F

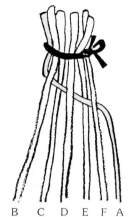

B C D E F A

2. Pass the leftmost strand **A** under **B**, over **C**, under **D**, over **E**, and under strand **F**.

C D E F A B

3. Pass the leftmost strand **B** under and over the strands to its right, including the end of strand **A**. The under/over pattern should alternate with that of the previous row.

D E F A B C

4. Repeat with strand **C**.

E F A B C D

5. Repeat with strand **D**.

F A B C D E

6. Repeat with strand **E**.

A B C D E F

7. Repeat with strand **F**.

new strand

8. When a strand runs out, lay a new one over the end of the old one so that the overlapped part passes under and over at least three other strands. Repeat steps 2 through 7 until the desired length is reached.

11

DYEING WITH ONION SKINS

Onion skin is one of the most readily available dyes around us. It contains a natural aniline dye. If you want to experiment with other vegetable dyes, see For Your Reference, page 142, for excellent books on the subject. Onion-skin-dyed raffia can be used in Project 5.

MATERIALS
10 oz (300 gm) of raffia, tied loosely in a bundle

3½ oz (100 gm) of brown onion skins (use Spanish or Bermuda onions)

½ gallon (2 liters) of water

EQUIPMENT
Two large enamel pots
Strainer
Rubber gloves
Drying stands/clothesline

INSTRUCTIONS

1. Soak the onion skins in water overnight in an enamel pot. Be sure to use enamel as the metals in other pots will cause chemical reactions that affect the dye.

2. Place the pot and its contents on a burner and simmer over low heat for one hour.

3. Strain the liquid into the other enamel pot. Discard the skins.

4. Add the loosely tied bundle of raffia to the liquid and simmer for 15 minutes. Leave the raffia in the pot until the liquid cools to room temperature.

5. Wearing the rubber gloves to keep your hands from absorbing the dye, wring the raffia to remove excess dyeing liquid and hang the bundle up to dry.

BASKETRY CONCEPTS ON THE MOVE

In the following discussion of the expressive potential of basketry, I have presented my personal approach as a contemporary Japanese basketmaker along with some of my baskets which demonstrate my expanded definition of the medium, my basic perception of space as a "second material," and my conceptualizing from the natural material. I have tried to make my personal standpoint clear in the hope that it will help you develop your own approach to the medium.

Slits from Scars
From the collection of K. Nakajo.

Mulberry bark, cherry bark; cut, stitched, and interlaced;
H 10″ (25.5 cm) × W 8″ (20.5 cm) ×
L 14″ (35.5 cm); 1984.

I have gradually come to accept my baskets being used in flower arranging. I find it does not subdue the independence of the work, and I am happy to be directly connected to a tradition that appreciates space.

To make this mulberry bark basket, I used cherry bark tapes and sewed several short pieces of wide mulberry bark into a long continuous sash. Then I interlaced the sash as if I were wrapping it around a ball of air. As the mulberry bark dried, slits formed and the edges of the slits curled, creating a mesh. The mesh gave the object the look of a woven structure. Now as I put the process of construction into words, it puzzles me that it all sounds too matter-of-fact and commonplace to be worthy of note. What excited me so much at the moment of discovery now sounds only natural when described along with the property of the material. So it seems that my whole "discovery," which seemed so dramatic to me then, was nothing more than what should happen according to the laws of nature. I had just been unable to see how nature worked until I made this basket. But I will continue to describe the process of discovery because what I have to say may show you another aspect of basketry.

Just before I started this basket, I was making a wrapped-air-ball basket with a long continuous sash of mulberry bark. I was having difficulties in hiding some lengthwise scars which had formed when the bark was removed from the trunk. The drier the bark got, the more pronounced the scars became, for the white edges of the scars curled over on the inside of the bark which I was using as the surface of the basket. So I covered them with mending stitches of cherry bark tape. But then, it suddenly occurred to me that I might use this property in some way. By opening the slits I could create patches of space in the bark, giving expression to an idea I had had for a long time: using holes or spaces in the textile structure as a secondary material. This idea came from my perception of vacant space not as the absence of material but as another kind of material, an intangible material. In this and other baskets, I have given equal weight to intangible and tangible materials.

Although I had not finished the basket with the scarred bark, I made a test model with slits like those on the basket shown. It was a thrill to watch how they turned out as the bark dried. I used this property of the material not only as the main theme of the basket but also applied it in finishing the edges of the sash. I folded the edges of the long sash over to the surface and slipped slender splits of bamboo between the folds as reinforcement. As the bark dried, the folded edge curled over the splits, making a perfectly proportioned, rounded border.

Exciting as this process of discovery was, I could have anticipated all this. In Basketry Basics, I stressed the relational aspects of basketry. I explained how the technique restricts the materials that can be used, how the material restricts the techniques that can be used, and how a form results from the subtle relationship between them. This is the primary rule of basketry. However, these restrictions do not have to confine the boundaries of imagination, but they do require an in-depth knowledge of the logic of nature. So rather than label these as restrictions, I would like to say that a material evokes a form and a method, and conceptualizing a form and a method reveals the properties of a material.

The following gallery of some of my recent baskets will, I hope, demonstrate the presence of these conceptual aspects in my work.

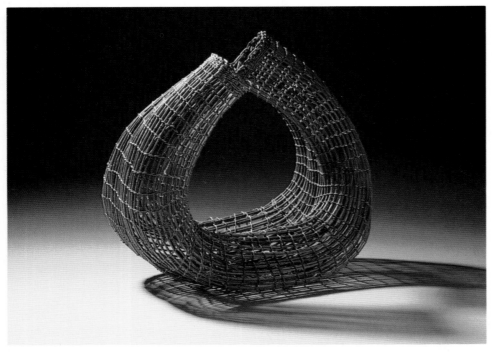

Space Encircled Space
Willow and rattan; twined;
H 11½″ (29.3 cm) × 11¾″ (29.7 cm) ×
D 6″ (15 cm); 1985.

A tubular basket of twined willow encircles inner space. The entire form is the result of many efforts to create a central hole and space within the tube. I planned the transparency of the wall so that it invites the viewer's eyes into the structure, and when light passes through, translates the basket form into a shadow.

Sashed Space
Sinomenine, ginger, iris; twined and interlaced;
H 8″ (20.5 cm) × D 10″ (25.5 cm); 1984.

A sphere of air is bound with a long sash of ginger and iris fronds twined around vine. The simple interlaced structure is the basic form of a three-dimensional textile.

Cut and Opened Hull
Sinomenine; looped; 8¼″ (21 cm); 1985.

Cutting shapes an object from a woven hull just as carving creates a shape out of solid wood. It is wonderful that a looped mass of sinomenine vine is flexible enough to open up to embrace a space within it and is solid enough to hold its shape.

Between Acts
Wisteria and sinomenine;
H 14½″ (37 cm) × W 17¾″ (45 cm) ×
D 8″ (20.5 cm); 1985.

An interlaced box of wisteria was cut in half on the diagonal and the two halves were turned around the axis and re-assembled. What is the back/front of the basket? What is the right/left? The top/bottom? What was cut? Just like the curtain rising to reveal a new set, each step brings another dimension and increases the complexity of the open space.

Lines with Width and Depth
Willow bark and branches; bound;
H 5″ (12.5 cm) × L 19″ (48.5 cm) × W 5″
(12.5 cm); 1985.

The natural structure of the willow branch suggested the form. The tape of willow bark connecting the branches forms lines and narrow planes as it twists and curls. These shifting forms give dimension to the bound space.

Twine-Bound Space
Paper mulberry bark; bound with hand-made twine; 8″ (20.5 cm); 1985.

Some elements have slipped, leaving only the binding twine in the original position. The independent space confined within the textile structure provides the image of a basket or package.

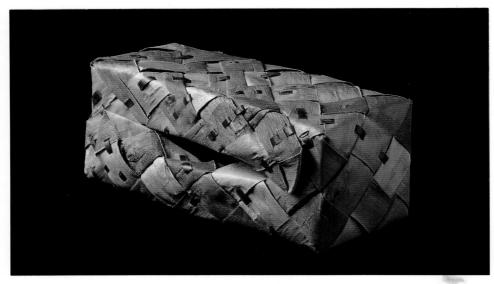

Hollow Solidity
Willow and cherry bark; plaited and sewn;
H 6″ (15 cm) × W 5½″ (14 cm) × L 13½″
(34 cm); 1985.

From the hidden interior a force lifts part of the form in an eddylike motion on the side of the basket. This makes the thin wall of willow bark look as if it was carved from wood and implies that the inner space is somehow full, not empty.

Two pieces of semi-cylindrical bark curled around the sides of a bamboo split basket as they dried. I allowed the bark to return to its natural shape and let the resilient inner basket fight against the embrace of the bark. The visual integrity is the result of the natural physical balance of the structural components.

Balanced V
From the collection of M. Matsubara.
Chamaecyparis sp. bark, *shinodake* splits, mulberry bark; plaited, tied;
H 12″ (30 cm) × W 7″ (18 cm) × D 4″ (10 cm); 1985.

Squarely Wrapped
Maple splint, cherry bark, dracaena;
plaited, twined, bent;
H 5″ (14 cm) × W 10½″ (26.8 cm) ×
L 10½″ (26.8 cm); 1984.

I wove a flat plane out of maple splints and dracaena fronds, and lifted and brought up the four corners of the plane to wrap inner space. A sense of the force that was used to bend the plane remains in the finished basket, a reminder of the wrapping technique I used and evidence of the resilience of the woven plane.

Cattail braid is woven with maple splints and sinomenine vine. Cattail has an interesting inner structure reminiscent of corrugated cardboard, with rows of raddles of fine fiber. Here its structure is reproduced in a basket pattern. The indented area suggests another form.

Indented
From the collection of R. Orton. Maple splint, cattail, sinomenine; woven;
H 13½″ (34.3 cm) × W 8″ (20.5 cm) × L 8″ (20.5 cm);
1984.

Hexagonal Openwork Basket
Willow and rattan; twined;
H 5″ (12.5 cm) × 13″ (33 cm); 1985.

Weaving round and round creates a continuous plane, which is emphasized by the regular repeating of bent lines. Although these lines create structural continuity, they break the visual continuity.

Even a Basket Rusts
From the collection of S. Takahashi.
Larch and cherry bark; joined and stitched;
H 4″ (10 cm) × W 8″ (20.5 cm) × L 8″ (20.5 cm); 1985.

This is a scrap of bark in the form of a basket. The surface appears rusted as if it were made from iron.

DIFFERENT PERSPECTIVES

At certain times in my life, casual contact with natural objects, folkcrafts, the works of contemporary artists, and even ordinary everyday objects or my own behavior have played a significant role in my approach to basketmaking, whether immediately or after a period of time. These contacts allowed me to break through my own conventionality and made me feel as if I had stepped through a gap in a hedge to find a totally different, new world on the other side of it. I have tried to explain each journey through the hedge in the notes before each of the five groups of projects.

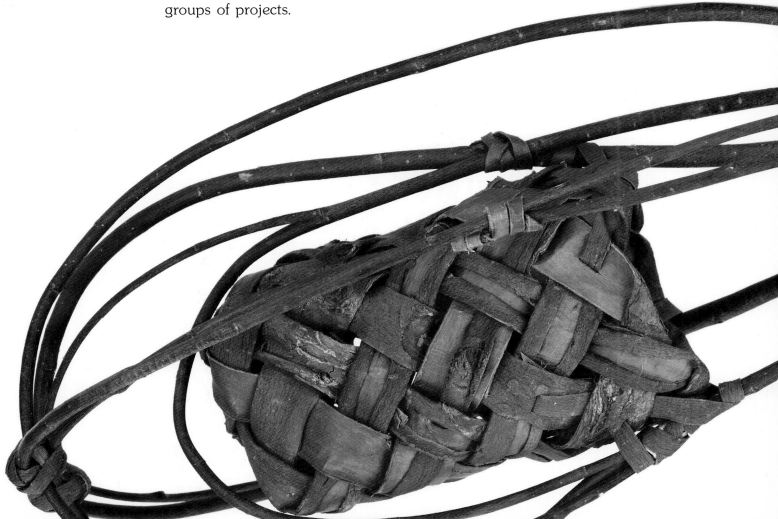

LEARNING FROM NATURE

While it is true that man creates form, it is also true that there are many shapes and forms already present in nature. The livistona water dipper from Okinawa shows what it is possible to do with a minimum of effort simply by making the most of what nature has to offer. The tip of a large livistona leaf is gathered, and bent back over its curved stem. Some strips of the leaf are wrapped around the gathered part and stem to form the handle.

Go outside and study the plants around you with a fresh eye and flexible mind. Try looking at them from a different angle or from close up. The new perspective will help you discover various interesting forms and shapes that will stimulate your creativity. Plants get their structures from the laws of nature and are therefore well-balanced and beautiful. Some of these structures can be used directly in basket construction. Instead of splitting a branch with a knife, try using naturally forked branches. Or make several splits in a stalk below a hard knob and use it as a ready-made knotted joint from which many spokes radiate.

Project 12 is based on my discovery of the attractive fan shape formed by the leaf of the windmill palm where it meets the stalk. Many stems have a naturally pleated leaf area right above the joint that is too lovely to be discarded. I hope this project will show you the delights of collaborating with nature.

Water dipper, Okinawa.

12

HANGING BASKET MADE FROM WINDMILL PALM STEM

This hanging basket makes the most out of the attractive natural fan shape of the leaf of the windmill palm. Simple of form and design, it can be made with just a palm leaf and some round reed or vine for a twining strand. Add a test tube and it becomes a flower vase.

MATERIALS

⅜″ (1 cm) × 14″ (35.5 cm) windmill palm (stem)
  Soak until the stem is flexible enough to be bent into a bow.

1/32″ (1 mm) #0 round reed or any kind of fine vine, 5′ (1.5 m)
  Soak for 10 to 20 minutes.

⅝″ (1.5 cm) × 6″ (15 cm) glass test tube

Hanging string

FINISHED SIZE: H 14¾″ (37.5 cm) × W 1⅛″ (2.8 cm)

EQUIPMENT

Single-edged or Swiss army knife
Piece of heavy leather
Flower arrangement shears

INSTRUCTIONS

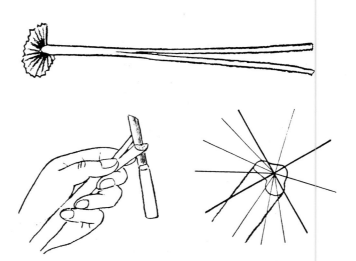

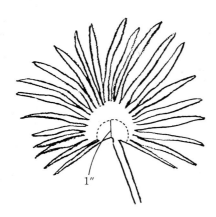

1. Cut out a small 1" (2.5 cm) fan shape from the leaf where it connects to the stem.

2. Split the stem (usually roughly triangular) in half lengthwise from the butt end up to a point 1½" (3.8 cm) from the joint. Using the illustration as a guide, gradually split the halves finer until you have ten to twelve spokes. Try to make each spoke equally thick.

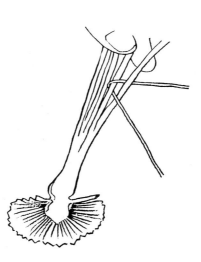

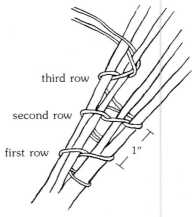

3. Use a knife to scrape off the pith from the inside of the spokes. Protecting your lap with heavy leather, lay the blade of your knife almost flat on the inside of the spoke and pull the spoke toward yourself.

4. Place the palm stalk with the fan-shaped part at the bottom and toward you. Bend the round reed in half and put the loop around a spoke in the front center.

5. Twine in a spiral to the right, leaving 1" (2.5 cm) space between rows. Keep the circumference from becoming too large by twining two spokes together when necessary. Twine three rows. After twining the last spoke in the third row, stop, and twine back to the first spoke. Twine back and forth, turning around at the center front three times. This forms an opening in the front of the palm stem.

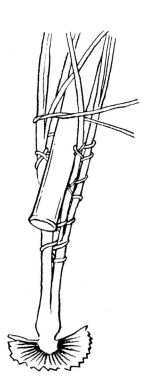

7. To reduce the circumference of the basket toward the bottom of the test tube, begin to twine adjoining spokes together.

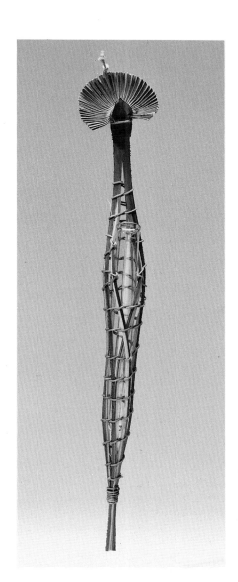

6. Insert the test tube at an angle, open end down, and twine spirally. Cross the two central spokes over each other. Keep twining.

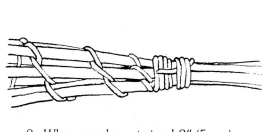

8. When you have twined 2″ (5 cm) past the bottom of the test tube, you will have only four or five groups of spokes. Clip off one of each pair. Cut off one of the twining strands and wrap the other around all of the spokes and over the end of the cut-off strand. After finishing, slide the end of the twining strand under the wrapped strand.

9. Tie a hanging string around the top of the basket, under the fan-shaped top.

FROM A TWO-DIMENSIONAL PLANE TO A THREE-DIMENSIONAL FORM

Generally, in basketry, space-containing form develops along with the basket wall: form emerges as the textile wall grows. This feature of basketry restricts expansion of the variety of forms. Would it be possible to get around this limitation by applying formation methods which are more commonly used with planal materials such as paper and leather?

Try this simple experiment that turns a two-dimensional plane into a three-dimensional form. Prepare a sheet of paper 4" (10 cm) × 8" (20.5 cm). Cut nine vertical, parallel slits lengthwise in the paper. Bring the two short ends together, and pull up and in on the two top corners. This will cause the slits to open up and create a curved bottom. The ten U-shaped strips embrace interior space, creating a three-dimensional form. This simple paper experiment forms the basis of the basket in Project 13.

This experiment shows how a form emerges the moment that a plane is bent around a space and thereby activates it. This made me start thinking about how I could involve space. Space can be regarded as one kind of material and is transformed more easily than any other real material for it is intangible. Bending a plane in this way allows for freer designs and different forms that cannot be achieved with other methods. The transformed plane retains traces of an applied force such as bending or folding and very success-fully conveys my intent to enclose space.

Creating baskets by bending or folding a plane is not a new idea, however. Project 14 is a typically formed tradi-tional Japanese winnowing basket, which is formed in almost the same way as a cardboard box is.

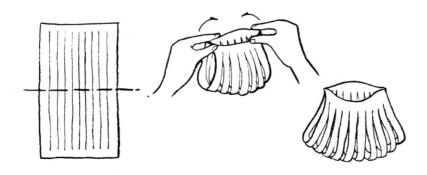

13

HANGING BASKET WITH CURVED BOTTOM

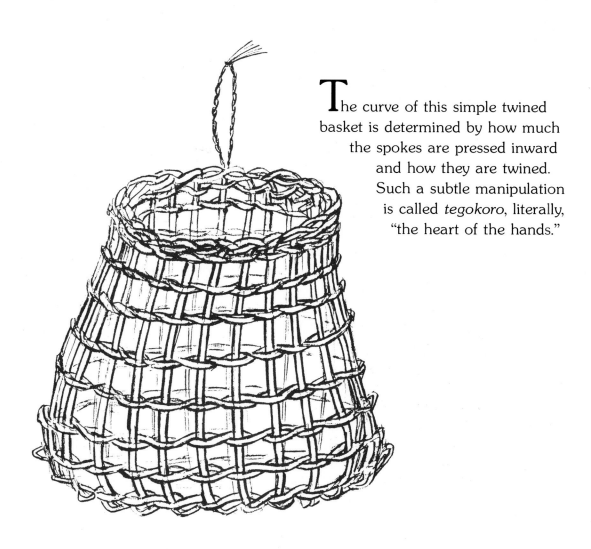

The curve of this simple twined basket is determined by how much the spokes are pressed inward and how they are twined. Such a subtle manipulation is called *tegokoro*, literally, "the heart of the hands."

MATERIALS

Any flexible twig or vine (sinomenine was used here)
  FOR SPOKES: ⅛" (3 mm) × 17" (43 cm), 11 strands
    The vine should be flexible enough to be bent into a ¾"
    (2 cm) diameter circle.
  FOR TWINING STRANDS: 1/16" (2 mm) × 23' (7 m)
    The vine should be more pliable than that used for the
    spokes.

If using sinomenine, soak for 3 hours.

FINISHED SIZE:
H 6¾" (17 cm) × W 6¾" (17 cm) × D 3½" (9 cm)

EQUIPMENT

Flower arrangement shears
Swiss army knife

INSTRUCTIONS

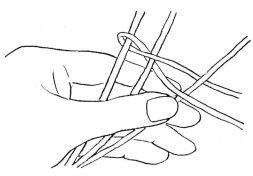

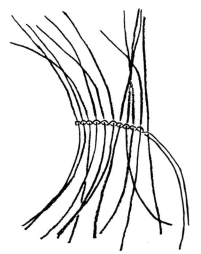

1. Hold several vertical spokes in your left hand, bend a twining strand in half around the center of the leftmost spoke, and twine the spokes together, leaving about ⅝" (1.5 cm) between spokes. Continue until you have twined all eleven spokes.

2. After twining, the spokes should be 6¾" (17 cm) wide. This line of twining will become the bottom of the basket.

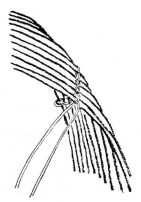

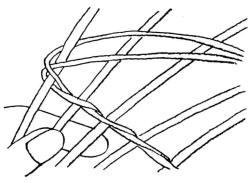

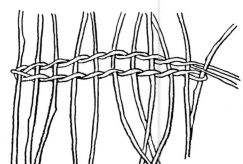

3. In order to twine left to right, flip the work over so the twining strands are to the left.

4. Bend the twining strands back and to the right, above the first row of twining.

5. Twine to the right, leaving 1" (2.5 cm) between the first and second rows at the middle of the work, to make the second row slightly curved.

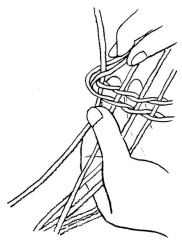

6. Flip the work over again to bring the twining strands to the left. Bend the twining strands back and to the right, above the beginning of the first row.

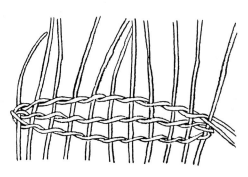

7. Twine to the right, curving the row as before.

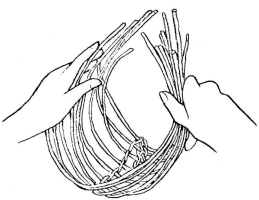

8. Grasp the ends of the spokes and fold the work in half, forming a U-shape.

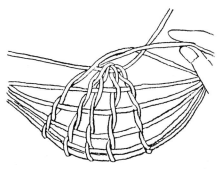

9. Hold the spokes in place, and twine the fourth and fifth rows to the right around the work, curving the rows as before.

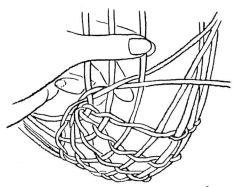

10. To deepen and round the basket bottom, bend the side spokes, and pull the twining strands tight at the beginning of the fourth, fifth, and sixth rows.

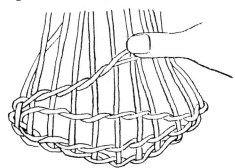

11. Curve these three rows so that they are next to each other at the sides of the basket and about 1″ (2.5 cm) apart in the middle. Pushing down on the middle spokes and out at both corners helps curve the bottom.

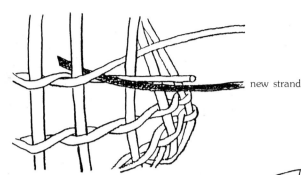

new strand

12. Joining twining strands should be done carefully in openwork. Working from the front of the basket, insert the new strand between the twining strands and behind a spoke.

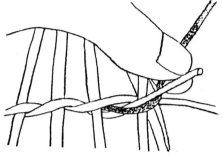

13. Twist the new strand around the old one.

14. Twine with the new strand. Tuck the end of the old strand under a spoke.

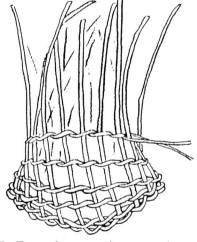

15. From the seventh row on, leave about the same amount of space between rows as you twine so the rows form horizontal, parallel lines. Twine the spokes closer together to gradually narrow the mouth of the basket.

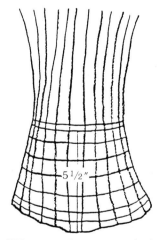

5½"

16. When you have twined 5½" (14 cm) from the first row, twine two rows close to each other to thicken the border. Cut off the twining strands and tuck the ends under the former row.

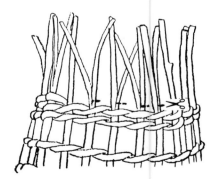

17. Split all of the spokes in half above the twining and cut off the right half of each.

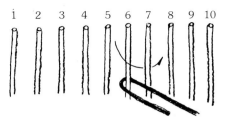

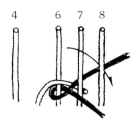

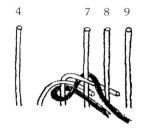

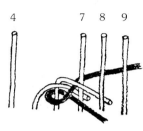

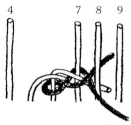

18. Split a 36" (91.5 cm) twining strand in half. Loop it around the sixth spoke from the left side, forming two twining strands. Bend the fifth spoke (from the left) to the right, in front of the sixth and behind the seventh. Then slip the front (left) twining strand over the bent spoke and behind the seventh spoke. Bend the sixth spoke (from the left) toward the right, in front of the seventh and behind the eighth spokes. Bring the twining strand in back of the spokes to the front between the seventh and eighth spokes. Cross the other twining strand over the strand and the bent spokes, and slip it behind the eighth spoke.

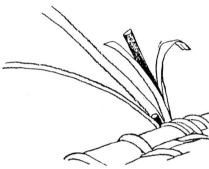

20. When you finish the row, carefully peel the bark from the core of the two twining strands, stopping at the basket border. Cut off the cores and use the two pieces of bark to make a hanging string.

19. Repeat step 18 until all the spokes are bent and caught between the twining strands.

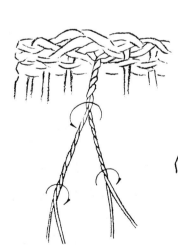

22. Tie a loop as shown to hang the basket.

21. Twist each strand of bark clockwise, then twist the two strands together counterclockwise into one piece of twine.

14

JAPANESE WINNOWING BASKET

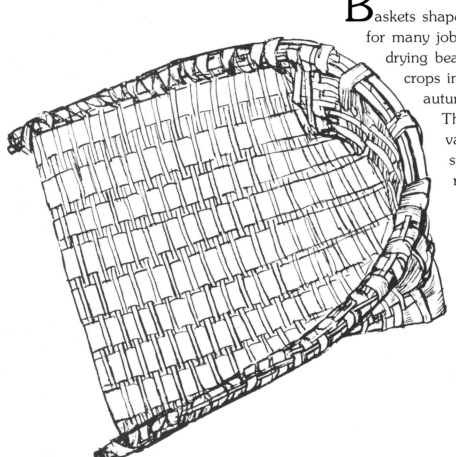

Baskets shaped like this have been used for many jobs besides winnowing: drying beans or vegetables, pouring crops into a bag, and gathering autumn leaves in the yard. The materials used also vary: maple splints, *matatabi* splits, bamboo splits, wisteria, and walnut bark.

MATERIALS

Bamboo splits   **See Project 8, page 54.**
FOR HORIZONTAL WEAVERS: ¼″ (6 mm) × 20″ (51 cm), 58 splits
FOR REINFORCEMENT: ¼″ (6 mm) × 17″ (43 cm), 5 splits
Soak for 15 minutes.

Strips of paper mulberry bark   **See Project 6, page 50.**
FOR BASKET BODY: 1½″ (3.8 cm) × 17″ (43 cm), 9 strips
FOR BORDER BINDER: ½″ (1.3 cm) × 8′ (2.5 m), 2 strips
Dip, and put in a plastic bag for 1 hour before using.

⅜″ (1 cm) × 24″ (60 cm), paper mulberry shoots,
  2 shoots
Soak for 1 day.

1¼″ (3.2 cm) × 5″ (12.5 cm) cherry bark, 3 strips
See Project 7, page 52.
Soak for 15 minutes.

FOR GUIDING NEEDLE:
¾″ (2 cm) × 7″ (18 cm) wood splint or bamboo split

FINISHED SIZE:
H ¾″ (2 cm) × W 13½″ (34.3 cm) × L 10½″ (26.8 cm)

EQUIPMENT

Flower arrangement shears
2 pieces of hemp string
Clothespins
Twist ties

INSTRUCTIONS

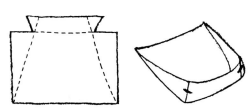

1. This winnowing basket is made flat, then folded and sewn at its corners.

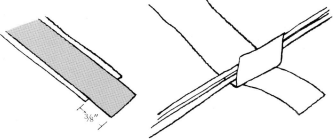

2. Lay three of the 17″ (43 cm) long strips of mulberry with the bark side down. Place the reinforcing cherry bark strips right side up on top of the mulberry, ⅜″ (1 cm) past the end. Turn the strips over with the doubled end toward you.

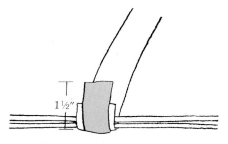

3. With the bark side of the mulberry facing up, place two bamboo splits, shiny side down, over one mulberry strip reinforced with cherry bark, about 1½″ (3.8 cm) from the cut edge. Fold the short end of the strip over the split.

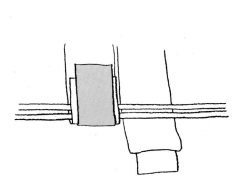

4. Slide another reinforced strip under the two bamboo splits and to the right of the first strip.

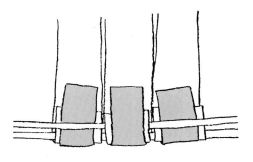

5. Fold 1½″ (3.8 cm) of the strip over the first bamboo split and under the second. Slip the third reinforced strip of bark under the bamboo to the left of the first strip of bark and fold it up in the same way.

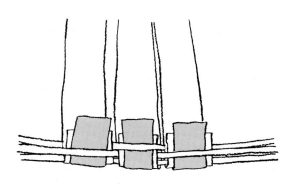

6. Weave in a third bamboo split so its under-one/over-one pattern alternates with the previous row.

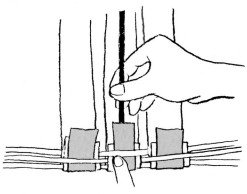

7. To reinforce the woven area, slip the ends of three of the wider bamboo splits under the folded strips.

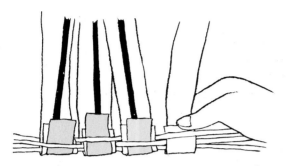

8. Fold up 1½" (3.8 cm) of six strips of mulberry and weave in three of the strips on each side of the initial three reinforced strips.

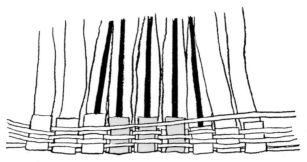

9. You should have nine strips altogether, with the cherry-bark-reinforced strips in the center. Add two more of the wider reinforcing bamboo splits vertically on both sides of the center three. Weave in five more bamboo splits.

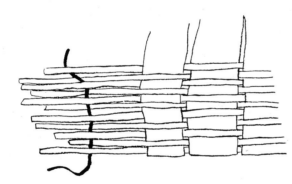

10. Turn your work over so the shiny, round side of the bamboo splits faces up. This side will become the inside of the basket. Weave a piece of hemp string into the bamboo splits parallel to the strips of bark. This string helps hold the weave tight.

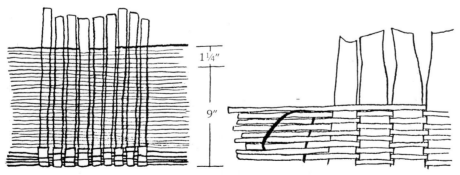

11. Continue weaving until the work measures 9" (23 cm). For the next 1¼" (3.2 cm), for a total length of 10¼" (26.2 cm), weave in bamboo splits with the rough side up. With the last bamboo split, weave only the center three strips of bark.

12. Cut off the end of the second strip from the left edge, leaving about 1½" (3.8 cm). (Save the bark cut off from the inner two strips for step 14.) Fold the end down on the side facing you and tuck it under the bamboo split of the previous row.

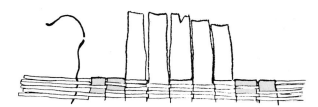

13. Cut and fold the next strip to the left in the same way, and insert the end under the third bamboo split from the top. Cut and fold the two strips on the right edge in the same way.

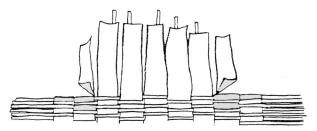

14. Place a short cut-off strip of bark on both sides of the five remaining strips. Fold the outer lower corners up diagonally.

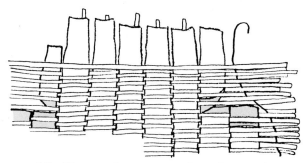

15. Weave nine more splits, shiny side down, into the 7 strips of bark. Place one more bamboo split, shiny side up, across the 7 strips. Cut off all but 1½" (3.8 cm) to 2" (5 cm) of the strips of bark.

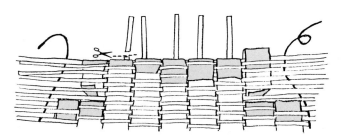

16. Fold them over the closest bamboo split and insert under the splits of previous rows. Clip the vertical reinforcing splits off even with the edge of the work.

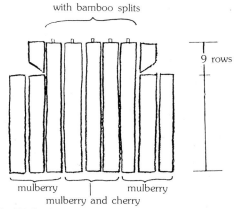

with bamboo splits

9 rows

mulberry   mulberry
mulberry and cherry

17. With the weaving finished, the work should look like this.

18. To finish the upper right edge of the work, take the lowest horizontal bamboo split that passes under the strip of bark and fold it up at right angles to the horizontal split above it. Pass it over this split and under the next.

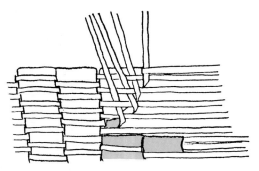

19. Fold up all the splits that pass under the strip on the upper right edge in the same way. Repeat the process with the upper left edge of the work.

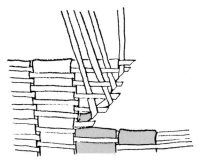

20. Cut off all the remaining bamboo splits even with this edge.

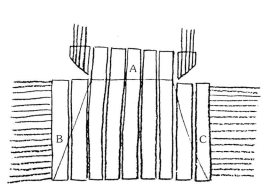

21. Bend the upper part of the work toward you along line **A**. Bend the flaps to the inside.

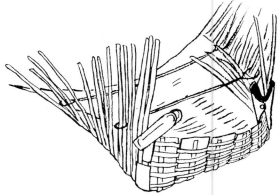

22. Fold up the sides along lines **B** and **C**. With the flaps inside, secure the corners with clothespins. Tying a piece of string across the middle of the basket should help hold the shape.

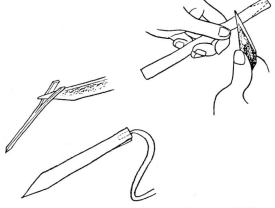

23. Make a guiding needle by whittling the end of the wood splint or bamboo split into a point. Make a 2″ (5 cm) split in the other end. Thread the needle by inserting bark in the split.

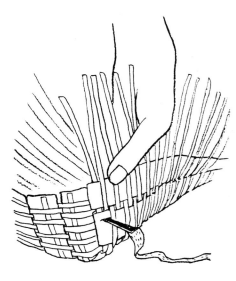

24. Sew the corners with the mulberry bark tape. From the outside of the corner, insert the needle into the lower strip of bark between the first and second vertical splits. Pull the needle through, drawing to the inside just enough bark to tie with.

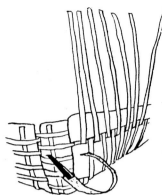

25. Attach the needle to the other end of the tape, and insert it into the vertical strip of bark just to the left of the vertical reinforcing split of bamboo. Pull the needle through.

26. Knot the two ends of the bark tape on the inside of the basket. The long end of the bark, which will be used to wrap the border, should be closest to the unfinished edge of the basket. Sew the other corner in the same way.

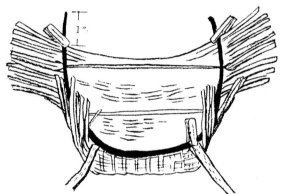

27. Place one of the mulberry branches along the inner edge of the basket border so it protrudes 1" (2.5 cm) past the end of the basket. Secure the branch with clothespins at the corners and the edges.

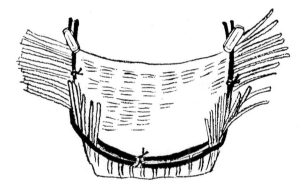

28. Place the other mulberry branch along the outer edge of the basket border and secure it with clothespins. To make the next few steps easier, attach twist ties at several places along the border and remove the clothespins.

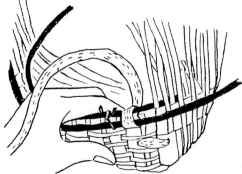

29. Attach the guiding needle to the long end of the bark tape inside the basket. Pull the tape straight up and wrap it around the inner and outer border branches, stitching through the woven bark strip.

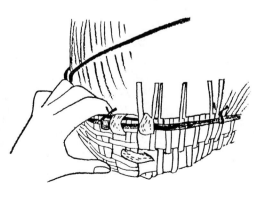

30. Make the second stitch to the right of the first vertical split. Cut the next two vertical splits in half and snip off the right half at the border. Trim the remaining half to 2" (5 cm). Cut off the next three vertical splits at the border. Repeat this reducing process with the rest of the vertical splits.

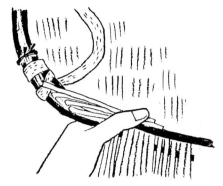

31. Bend the splits down and to the right as shown.

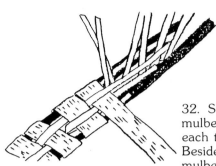

32. Stitch around the border, passing the mulberry tape under one of the bent splits each time, thus making a border pattern. Besides being decorative, this will keep the mulberry bark tape from coming completely unravelled when part of the border gets worn out.

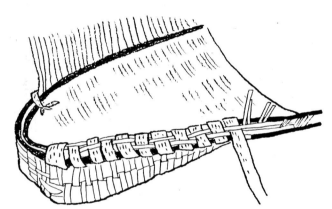

33. Stitch until you come to the front edge of the basket, remove the needle and stitch the other side of the border following steps 29 through 32.

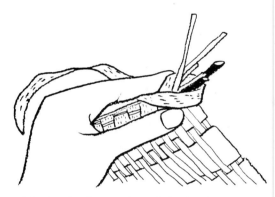

34. At the front edge of the basket, wrap the mulberry tape around the ends of the branches several times as shown.

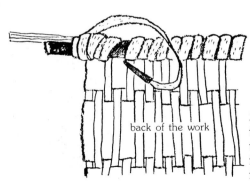

back of the work

35. Bring the tape to the back of the work and stick the needle through the bark between the fourth and fifth splits from the front edge. Pull the needle through to the other side.

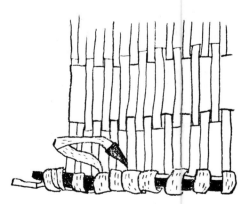

36. Pierce the bark between the seventh and eighth splits from the edge and pull the needle through to the back.

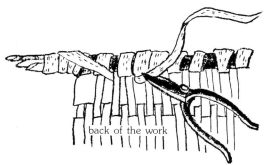

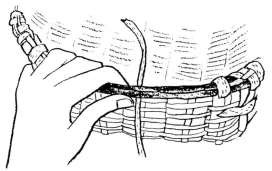

37. Clip off the mulberry bark tape. Use the leftover bark to bind the center of the border. Repeat from step 34 for the other side of the border.

38. Pierce the bark at the center to the left of the vertical reinforcing split.

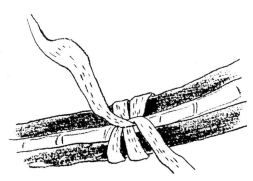

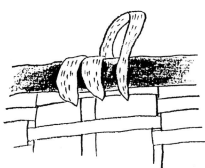

39. Wrap the bark tape around twice and twist the two ends together on the inside of the basket. To finish the ends, pierce the bark under the border once more and weave the ends into the bamboo splits.

RESPONDING TO THE PROPERTIES OF MATERIALS

Have you ever had to give up a design when the material you were using turned out to be incompatible with the construction method? I know from thousands of such experiences how discouraging it is. But I also know the happiness that can result from such experiences. When the solution is found, the struggle involved in overcoming the problem adds meaning and enjoyment to the work.

All materials have their own special properties and characteristics just as people do. If we can stop thinking of materials as good or bad, we can respond to their inherent qualities and deal with problems more easily.

There are three ways to treat materials. The first is to transform the available material to a shape or form that suits the method of construction. For example, in Project 15, weak cattails were braided to make them the equivalent of wide splints, and rigid maple wood is split into more manageable flat tape.

The second is to combine complementary materials and use them as one material. In the willow and birch coiled basket of Project 4, I blended materials to create another kind of material and, at the same time, solve a shortage of materials.

The third way is to alter or transform the technique to fit the material, which often results in the dramatic conversion of a problem into the discovery of a new concept. Suppose the material is too short. Think what could be done if you use it with some other technique that might take advantage of the shortness. In the short-strand coiling of Project 16, the corn husk mat, the short husks are first used as binders, then they become the foundation of the coil itself as new binders are added. This exciting technique, common among traditional Japanese rice straw basketry, demonstrates the wisdom of basketmakers in matching technique to material.

So the real essentials of good basketry seem not to be the properties we demand of materials but the flexible minds we, as basketmakers, must have.

15

CATTAIL BRAID
AND MAPLE
SPLINT BASKET

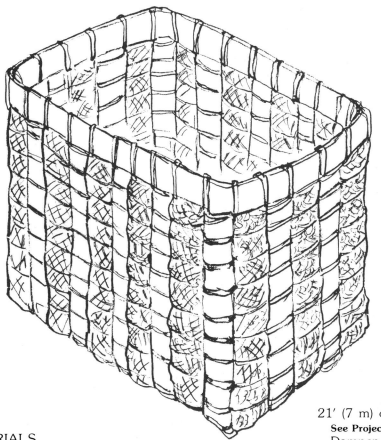

<W>hen weaving with an even number of warps, letting one strand chase the other creates a vertically aligned pattern. The sinomenine vine looks like a ladder, and the cattail braid enhances the vertical continuity.

MATERIALS

$\frac{1}{32}$" (1 mm thick) × $\frac{5}{8}$" (1.5 cm) maple splints
See Project 9, page 57.
FOR BODY OF BASKET:
24" (61 cm), 5 splints
20" (51 cm), 10 splints
FOR BORDER: 26" (66 cm), 2 splints

Soak for about 30 minutes.

30' (9 m) of $\frac{1}{16}$" (2 mm) fine vine
Sinomenine was used here for its black color.
Soak the vine for 2 to 3 hours.

21' (7 m) of $\frac{5}{8}$" (1.5 cm) six-strand cattail braid
See Project 10, page 60.
Dampen the braid before weaving.
SUBSTITUTES: iris, sedge, grass, or lily, either singly or combined

FINISHED SIZE:
H 6½" (16.3 cm) × W 5½" (14 cm) × L 8¼" (21 cm)

EQUIPMENT

Flower arrangement shears
Swiss army knife
Clothespins
Twist ties

INSTRUCTIONS

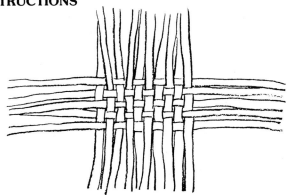

1. Lay the ten shorter splints side by side vertically and, through the center, weave the five longer splints under and over them at a right angle. The rectangular woven section should measure 7½" (19 cm) by 4" (10 cm).

2. The first twining strand should measure at least two and a half times the distance around the woven area (enough for two rows) when folded in half. Loop the folded end of the vine around the fifth splint from the upper left. Working toward the right, do one row of twining around the woven area.

3. With the woven area top side down, stand all the splints up at a right angle to the bottom and do the second row of twining, holding the splints in place as you twine.

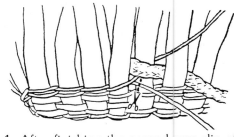

4. After finishing the second row, clip off one twining strand in front of a splint and tuck the end under the previous row. Insert the braid above the clipped end of the twining strand as shown.

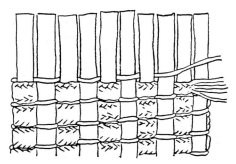

5. Now weave a row under-one/over-one with the braid and then with the vine for 10 rows. Since there is an even number of splints, on every other splint you have rows of braid or lines of vines.

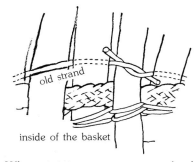

6. When joining a new strand of vine, twist the two ends around each other on the inside of the basket.

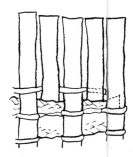

7. End the weaving at a corner. To make the border level, the braid must be tapered. Unravel the braid, then rebraid it tighter, gradually reducing the number of strands. Slip the end into the previous row. End with a final row of vine.

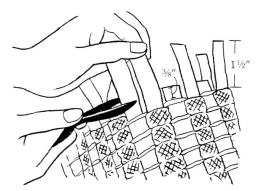

8. To finish the border of the basket, cut off all but 1½″ (3.8 cm) of the splints under the vertical rows of braid and all but ⅜″ (1 cm) of those under the rows of vine.

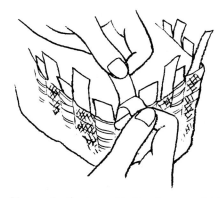

9. Use a knife to split the layers of the longer splints. Pull them apart.

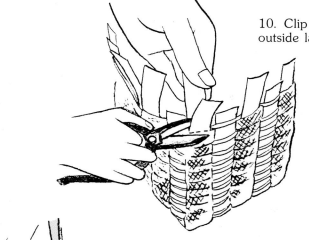

10. Clip off all but ⅜″ (1 cm) of the outside layer of each splint.

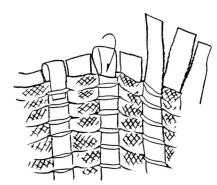

11. Slip the inner layer of each splint under the second vine from the top row on the inside of the basket.

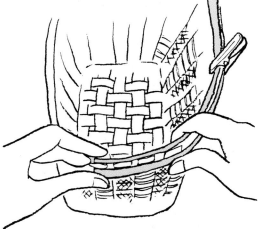

12. Place one 26″ (66 cm) splint around the outside and another splint of the same length around the inside of the border. Hold the splints in place with clothespins.

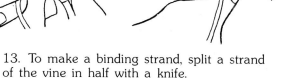

13. To make a binding strand, split a strand of the vine in half with a knife.

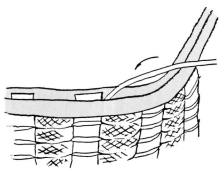

14. With the outside of the basket toward you, stick the tip of the binding strand between the two horizontal border splints. The flat back of the strand should face you.

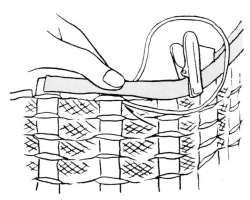

15. From the outside, stick the other end of the binding strand under the top row of vine and to the right of a visible vertical splint. Pull the strand through to the inside. Repeat. The end of the binding strand should be inside the basket.

16. From the inside, insert the end of the binder to the left of the next visible vertical splint to the right, and above the top row of braid. Pull it through. The binder strand makes a horizontal line inside the basket.

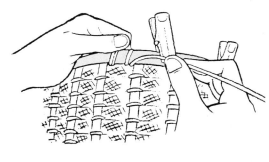

17. Wrap the strand around the splints once and bring the end out in the same place. Then insert it to the right of the same vertical splint from the outside. Wrap once and move to the right on the inside just as in step 16. Bind all the way around the border.

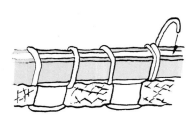

18. When you reach the first stitch, the end of the strand should be on the inside of the basket, Pull it up and insert it between the two border splints.

16

SHORT-STRAND
COILED MAT

W hen a strand is twisted tightly,
it twists over itself and makes a loopy
knot. Here this property is used to
hold the binder in the short-strand
coiling of this project.
It is really too simple to be
called a technique.

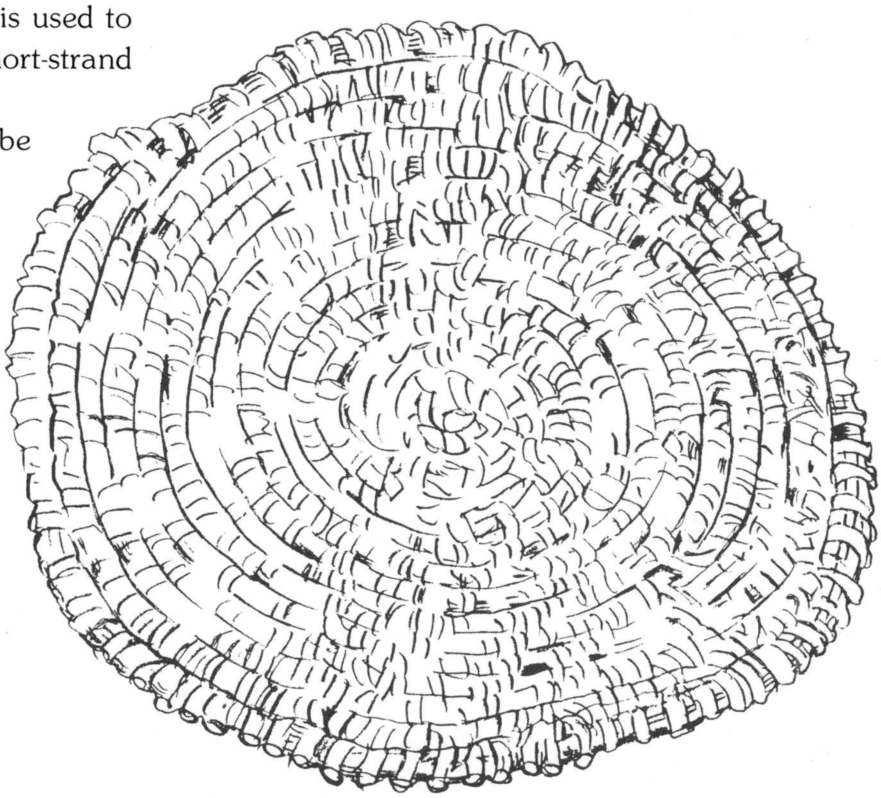

MATERIALS

7 oz (200 gm) dried corn husks
  Dip the husks in water for one minute, drain well, and wrap
  them in a towel. Remove the stiff ends and split the
  husks in half or in thirds.

FINISHED SIZE: D 12" (30 cm)

EQUIPMENT

Scissors

INSTRUCTIONS

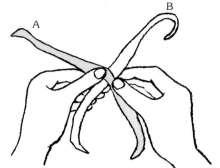

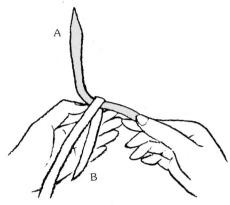

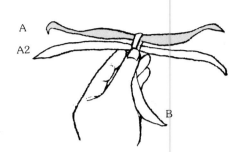

1. Cross corn husk **A** over **B**.

2. Fold **B** over **A**. Turn so **A** is horizontal.

3. Place another husk **A2** under both layers of the folded corn husk.

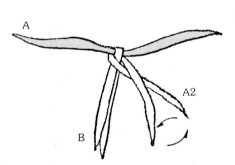

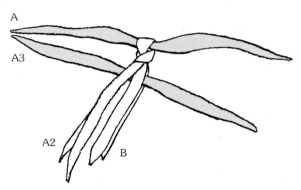

4. Bring the two ends of corn husk **A2** up around the folded corn husk. Twist the ends together very tightly so that corn husk **A** is secured between folded husk **B**.

5. Bring the twisted ends of **A2** down on the top of **B** and insert another corn husk **A3** horizontally between the two folded halves of **B**.

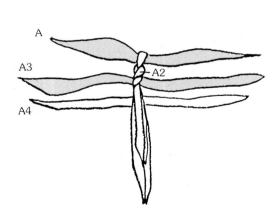

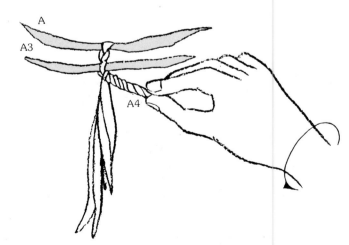

6. Place corn husk **A4** under the vertical coil bundle and bring its ends over the bundle and twist them together.

7. The ends of corn husk **A4** should be twisted tight to secure the twisted ends of corn husk **A2** in the bundle.

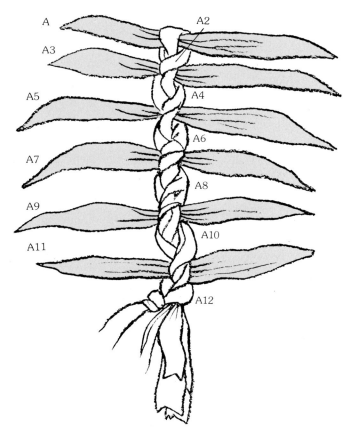

8. Keep adding crossing husks and twisting husks until you have six crossing husks and six twisted knots.

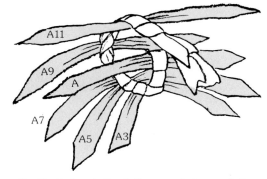

9. Curl the tail of the work toward the starting point, making a small ring. The twisted knots should be on the outside.

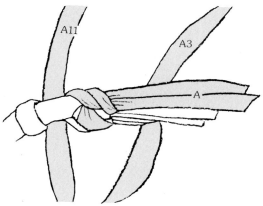

10. Place the end of the tail between the ends of the first crossing husk **A**. Tightly twist the ends of **A** together, and place them on top of the tail.

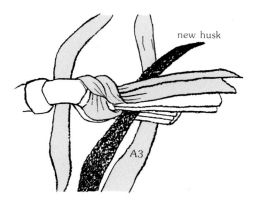

11. Place a husk under the bundle of twisted ends and add a couple of strands to the bundle to lengthen it. Then bring the ends of the next crossing husk **A3** around the bundle and twist them.

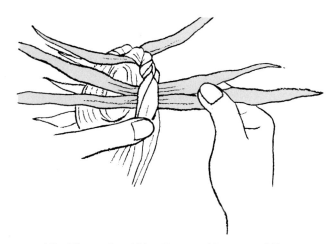

12. There should be 7 twisted knots and 5 crossing husks in the first row.

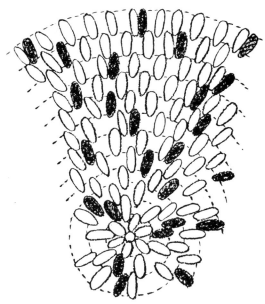

13. As the mat gets larger, increase the number of husks by securing two crossing husks at once. Increase the number of crossing husks as follows.

Second row: Add one husk every other husk.
Third through sixth rows: Add one every third husk.
Seventh and eighth rows: Add one every fourth husk.
Ninth through twelfth rows: Add one every fifth husk.
Subsequent rows: Increase at roughly even intervals, adding enough so the mat lies flat.

14. Continue until the mat measures 12″ (30 cm). Do not add crossing husks in the last row; simply twist the ends of the husks of the previous row and add them to the coil bundle. When you reach the last crossing strand, twist each end, and tie them together. Cut off the coil bundle.

Hanging basket with curved bottom, Project 13, page 83; Hanging basket made from windmill palm stem, Project 12, page 79; Japanese winnowing basket, Project 14, page 88. ▶

Plaited basket in a free-form willow basket, Project 17, page 110; Cattail braid and maple splint basket, Project 15, page 97; Short-strand coiled mat, Project 16, page 101; Bamboo screen with weighted bobbin twining, Project 18, page 115; Grass slippers, Project 19, page 119.

DEVICES THAT MAKE THINGS POSSIBLE AND EASIER

Usually the novice learns basketmaking techniques by copying conventional baskets with traditional materials. The details and methods of construction are so well thought out and the materials used so appropriate that innovation seems impossible. Thus it is very easy to get trapped into blind acceptance of these rules and traditions. As long as the basketmaker follows conventions, he will not be able to produce anything but traditional forms. Try to break the rules and go beyond traditions.

Once you have passed this initial barrier, I am afraid you will soon find that the real difficulty does not lie in breaking the rules but in solving the technical problems which suddenly emerge as if taking their revenge on you for disregarding the rules. But it is also challenging to discover a solution. I once slipped cherry bark tape between the folds of a small piece of cherry bark and used it as a guiding needle, making it possible for me to stitch through layers of bark easily, even from the inside of the basket.

Constructing a maquette (a small preliminary model) will make it easier for you to envision the project and deal with any technical difficulties. The basket in Project 17 was plaited with three continuous strips, eliminating the turned-over edges usually found at the borders of plaited baskets. I got the idea when I was looking at the laminated cardboard box my husband's Scotch whisky came in. It was wrapped diagonally with one ribbon. Then I remembered that John McQueen had suggested using a mold in his workshop at Peter's Valley Craft Center. I found that at that time I did not realize the significance of his suggestion, and only understood it as a way to make it easier to manipulate fiber. Looking at this box, I realized what he really meant was that trying an idea out with a maquette would be a good way to experiment with new forms.

In the bamboo screen of Project 18, weighted bobbins hold numerous twining strands in position. In Project 19 the body acts as a loom. Using devices to manipulate materials and not relying only on our hands relates basketry to loom weaving and breaks with conventional concepts of what is moved and how the fibers are kept in position.

◄ A string of peppers, Project 20, page 127; Rice cakes wrapped in dwarf bamboo leaves, Project 21, page 130; Protective snow cap for plants, Project 22, page 133; Wrapped eggs, Project 23, page 137.

17

PLAITED BASKET IN A FREE-FORM WILLOW BASKET

This right-angle plaiting technique creates a neat border by reducing the number of strips that must be folded down at the basket border. If this basket were made in the usual manner with eight strips, there would be sixteen folds at the border, but with this technique the same form is created with three strips, and so there are only eight folds at the border.

MATERIALS

Willow bough with several branches, large enough to enclose an oblong inner basket of 6¾" (17 cm) × 2¾" (7 cm) × 2¾" (7 cm)

Soak the bough for 3 days until it is perfectly flexible.

1" (2.5 cm) strips of willow bark
strip **A**, 6' 6" (2 m)
strips **B** and **C**, 4' (1.2 m) each

See steps 1 and 2 for how to estimate the necessary length for your basket.

See step 3 before cutting if the thickness of the bark varies greatly.

Soak for 1 hour and use a knife to scrape the knotty thick parts on the outside of the bark. Cut into strips after soaking.

5' (1.5 m) of ¼" (6 mm) strips of willow tape

FINISHED SIZE: H 22" (56 cm) × W 8" (20 cm) × D 7¾" (19 cm)

EQUIPMENT

Flower arrangement shears
10" (26 cm) × 17¼" (44 cm) stiff cardboard
Clothespins
Single-edged knife
String
Twist ties
Hammer
¼" (6 mm) nails
Alcohol burner or gas range burner

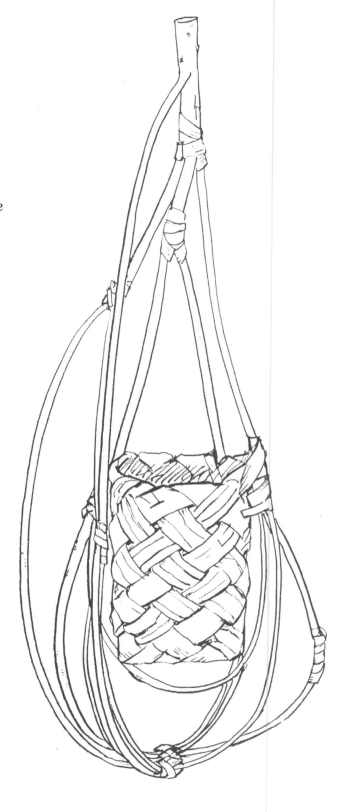

INSTRUCTIONS

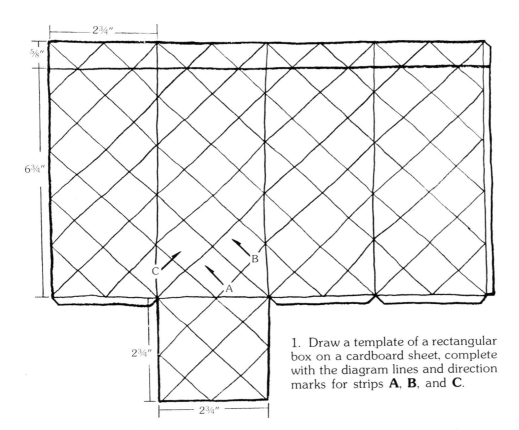

2¾"

⅝"

6¾"

C

B

A

2¾"

2¾"

1. Draw a template of a rectangular box on a cardboard sheet, complete with the diagram lines and direction marks for strips **A**, **B**, and **C**.

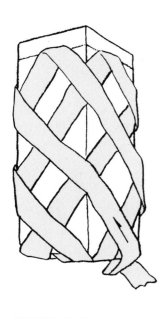

2. Cut the template out and make the box. To estimate how much bark you will need for strips **A**, **B**, and **C**; wrap a 1″ (2.5 cm) strip of paper around the box, starting at the marked points in the indicated directions and following the diagram lines. Fold the strips of paper around the corners and fold under and back at the top line. Strips **B** and **C** are the same length. Add 4″ (10 cm) to the length of the paper strip to allow for the length consumed in folding the thick bark around the corners and for the overlap at the end of the strip.

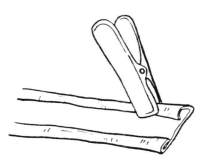

3. If the thickness of the bark varies too greatly, make each strip 1½″ (3.8 cm) wide and fold both edges of the strips toward the inside of the strip. The folded strip should be 1″ (2.5 cm) wide. This compensates for the thinness and also provides textural contrast between the back and front.

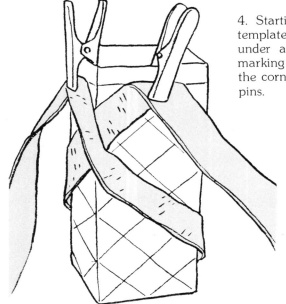

4. Starting at the point marked **A** on the template, wrap strip **A** around it, folding under and back at the horizontal line marking the border and folding around the corners. Secure the strips with clothespins.

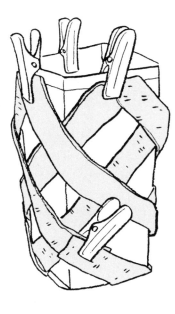

5. When strip **A** comes back to the beginning, overlap the ends and hold with a clothespin. When wrapping toward the basket border, strip **A** goes over itself; when wrapping down toward the basket bottom, under.

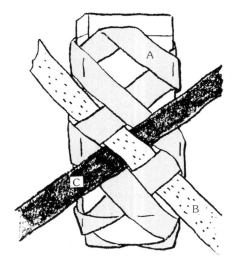

6. Plait in the beginning of strips **B** and **C** at the same time. Wrap strip **B** all the way around, crossing under **A** and over itself when plaiting toward the border, and over **A** and under itself when plaiting down. Finish plaiting strip **C**, crossing over **A**, under **B**, and under itself when plaiting up; and under **A**, over **B** and over itself when plaiting down.

7. Remove the clothespins. Dry the finished basket on the template until the bark is dry enough to hold its shape but still pliable enough to be slit with a knife without cracking. These slits will be used in fastening the plaited basket to the outer basket (see step 13).

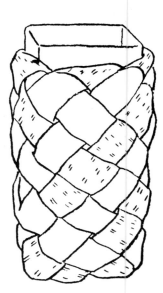

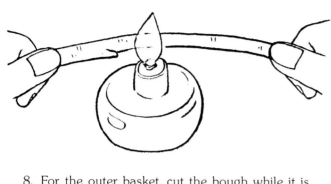

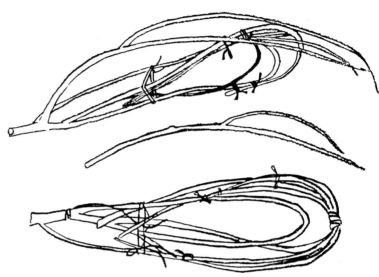

8. For the outer basket, cut the bough while it is wet into two or three parts so it can be reshaped into a fuller bough to hold the inner basket. To curve the branches, hold the branch in the flame of an alcohol burner, turning the branch and moving it back and forth. The heat will make it flexible enough to be bent with your hands. Warm the branch at several places along each curve.

9. Arrange the curved branches in the desired shape and fasten them to each other temporarily with string or twist ties.

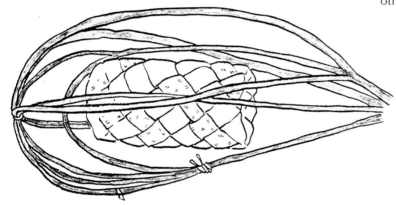

10. To determine the best position for the branches, put the plaited basket inside. Taper the tips of the branches and nail them in place.

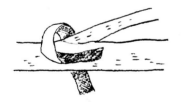 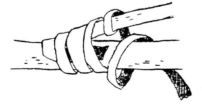 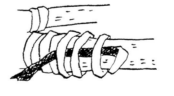 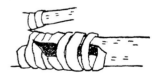

11. Secure the branch tips with bark, wrapping from the lowest point of the joint. Place one end of the bark so it will be under the wrapping. With the other end, wrap around the joint several times, then wrap around the thinner branch once or twice before returning to wrap around the thicker branch again. Slip the end of the bark under the last three or four wrappings.

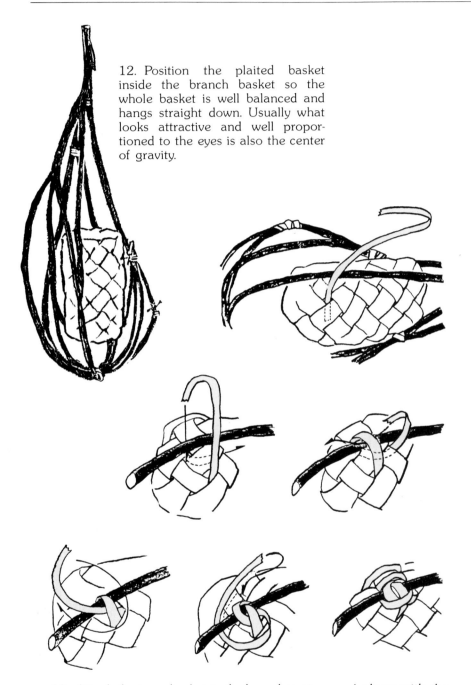

12. Position the plaited basket inside the branch basket so the whole basket is well balanced and hangs straight down. Usually what looks attractive and well proportioned to the eyes is also the center of gravity.

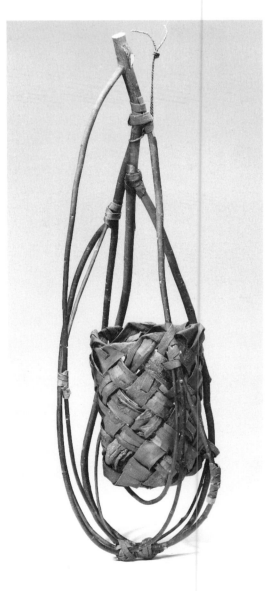

13. Attach the inner basket to the branches at several places with the ¼″ (6 mm) willow tape. Make slits in the strips of plaiting if necessary (see step 7). Bring the tape to the outside of the basket using a slit or opening in the plaiting. Pass the tape over the branch and under part of the plaiting. Bring it to the outside somewhat higher than at first. Pass it under the previous stitch, over the branch, and wrap it around under the branch. Insert the end into the plaiting and draw it out on the inside again. Finish the ends of the tape by stitching them into the plaiting and cutting them off inside the basket.

18

BAMBOO SCREEN WITH WEIGHTED BOBBIN TWINING

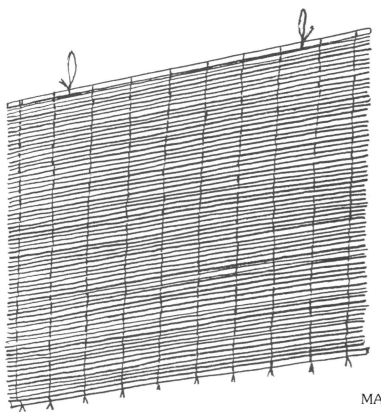

A bamboo screen shuts out sunlight and heat, and protects you from the intruding eyes of people passing by. In the Japanese culture, where a strand of twine, or *shimenawa*, keeps out trespassers, divisions of space seem to be mental rather than physical boundaries. Weighted bobbin twining is one of the ancient Japanese weaving methods that have been used extensively since the Neolithic Age to make fish traps, rush mats, straw barrels to hold rice, and burden bags.

MATERIALS

Bamboo splits (surface of large stalk of bamboo works best)
See Project 8, page 54.
FOR BODY OF SCREEN: $\frac{1}{16}$" (2 mm thick) × $\frac{1}{16}$" (2 mm) × 26" (66 cm), 150 splits
FOR TOP AND END SPLITS: $\frac{1}{16}$" (2 mm thick) × $\frac{3}{8}$" (1 cm) × 26" (66 cm), 2 splits

$\frac{1}{16}$" (2 mm) tightly spun cotton string
FOR TWINING STRANDS: 3' (1 m), 10 strands
FOR HANGING STRINGS: 12" (30 cm), 2 strands

FINISHED SIZE: W 26" (66 cm) × L 20" (51 cm)

EQUIPMENT

Flower arrangement shears
4" (10 cm) or 1 oz (30 gm) bolts, 20
$\frac{3}{4}$" (2 cm) × 2" (5 cm) × 4' (1.2 m) piece of lumber
Two trestles or stools
Saw

INSTRUCTIONS

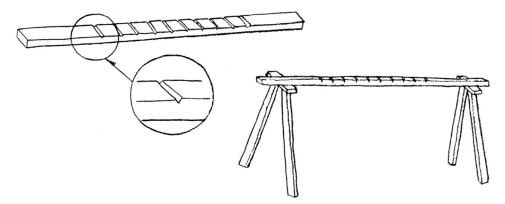

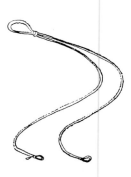

1. With the saw, cut ten grooves at 2¾" (7 cm) intervals across the horizontal bar. Place the ends of the bar on the two trestles.

2. Fold each of the 10 strands of string in·half, tie a slip knot in the middle, and knot each end.

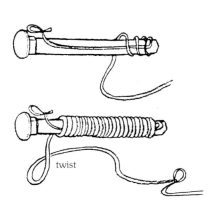

3. Holding the knotted end of one strand near the head of the bolt, lay the string down the length of the bolt, and wrap the string around the bolt as shown. When you have wrapped 12" (30 cm) of string around the bolt, make a loop and twist it.

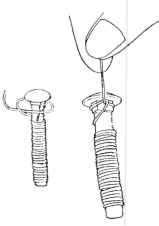

4. Slip the twisted loop over the head of the bolt and tighten it. The bolt should hang down without the string unravelling.

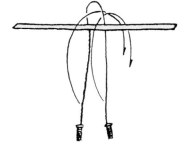

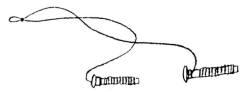

5. Repeat steps 3 and 4 with the other end of the string and the rest of the strands.

6. Untie the slip knot in the middle of the string. Pull the string over the center of the shiny side of one of the wider bamboo splits as shown and then slip the two bolts through the loop. This will become the top split of the screen.

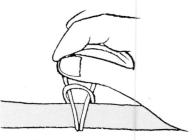

7. Pull the string tight.

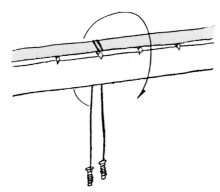

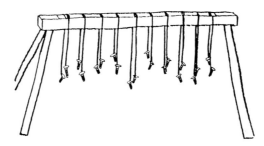

8. Place the split on the horizontal bar, right side up, and center it over the ten grooves. The two ends of the string should hang down on the far side of the bar. Slide the string until it is aligned with one of the grooves in the bar. Lift one bolt (bobbin) over the split and bring it toward you. Let it hang.

9. Repeat steps 6 through 8 with the rest of the bobbins. Each string should be aligned with a groove in the horizontal bar.

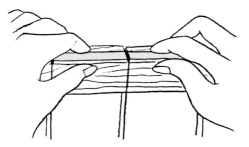

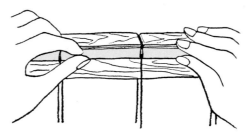

10. Slide the top split off the bar, slipping the strand into the groove.

11. Lay the split against the side of the bar as shown.

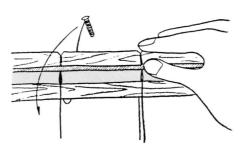

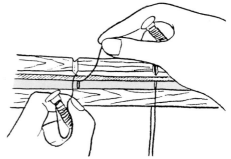

12. Place a fine split, right side up, on the top of the horizontal bar, above the top split and over the strand hanging down in back. Pick up the back strand with your left hand and the front one with your right hand.

13. Bring the strand in your left hand to the front over the split and lift the one in your right hand over the split and behind the bar. The fine split is now between the two strands. Repeat with all ten strings. Always pick up the back and front strands with the same hand or the two strands will not be properly twined.

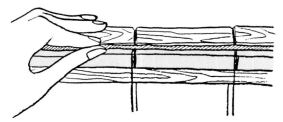

14. Add fine splits one by one.

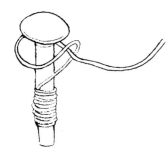

15. When you start to run out of twining strand, release the loop around the head of the bolt and unwind the string. Make a loop with the end of the string and slip it around the head of the bolt.

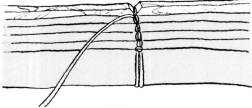

16. Twine all 150 fine splits.

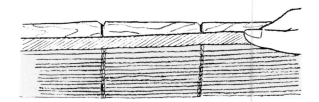

17. Add the end split, right side toward you.

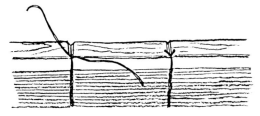

18. Tie knots in the strands on the upper edge of the end splint. This is the bottom of the bamboo screen. Cut the strings off.

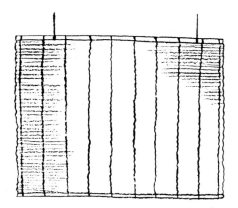

19. Attach two strings on both sides of the top split to hang the screen.

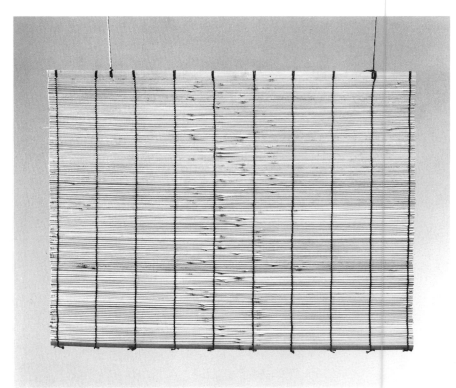

19

GRASS SLIPPERS

These grass slippers were traditionally made of rice straw and worn outdoors. They wore out fast, and when they were part of everyday wear, even children had to make pair after pair. Cultures that depend or have depended on perishable materials like grass, rice straw, or wood instead of longer-lasting materials are likely to develop different values, especially those concerning labor and possessions.

MATERIALS

7 oz (200 gm) soft rush (*Juncus* sp.)
Moisten to use.
SUBSTITUTES: tule, rice straw, esparto

¾″ (2 cm) strips of cotton, 10′ (3 m)

FINISHED SIZE: W 4½″ (11.5 cm) × L 9½″ (24.3 cm)

EQUIPMENT

Flower arrangement shears
3′ (1 m) cord for back strap
Piece of cardboard larger than your foot (for template)
Guiding needle **See Project 14, step 23, page 92**.
Wooden mallet and base
Wooden stand (or your toes)

INSTRUCTIONS

1. Using 12 to 16 stems of rush, make enough twine to reach from hand to hand of your outstretched arms. This length is for one slipper and differs for each person. This twine is used as the warp strands.

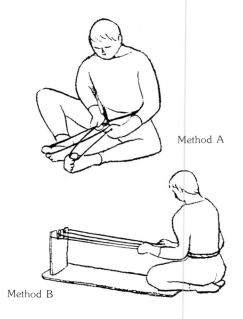

Method A

Method B

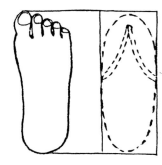

2. Trace around your foot on the cardboard. Draw a simplified oval shape a little smaller than your foot. Compare this template with your work as you weave.

3. There are two ways to hold the warp twine for weaving. For Method A, sit on the floor with your knees bent and your feet in front of you. Loop the warp twine around your toes and wrap the back strap around your waist (see step 4). For Method B, build a three-pronged stand out of wood. Loop the warp twine around the prongs of the stand and the back strap around your waist (see step 4).

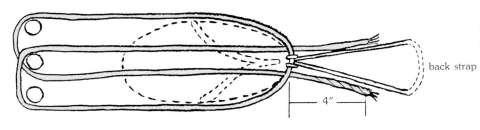

back strap

4"

4. For both methods, the warp twine is placed as shown. The warp twine appears to be much longer than the finished slipper but this extra length disappears when the loose ends of the warp twine are pulled in steps 21 through 23. Loop the twine around your toes or the prongs, and tie the back strap onto the twine.

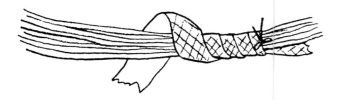

5. To decorate and reinforce the nose of the slipper, wrap 8 to 10 stems of rush with the fabric strip until you have covered 12" (30 cm).

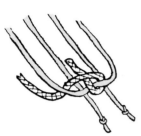

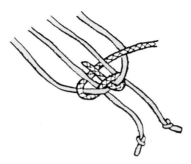

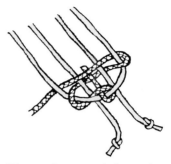

6. Place the fabric-wrapped strand in the center of the warp twine at the nose of the slipper and wrap the long end over and under the twine, then over itself, and under the left edge of the twine.

7. Pass the strand back to the right over the leftmost warp twine, under the two middle warp twines and itself, then over the twine on the right.

8. Weave the strand through again, reversing the under/over pattern of the previous row.

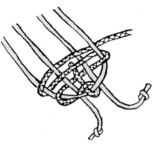

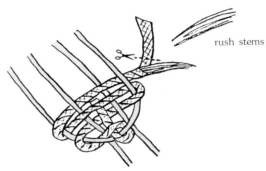

rush stems

9. Weave it through once more in an under-one/over-one pattern.

10. To continue weaving, add 5 to 6 more stems of rush to the center of the fabric-wrapped strands and cut away the wrapping fabric.

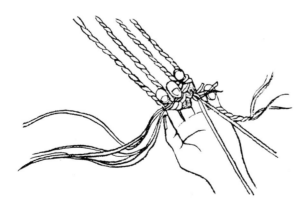

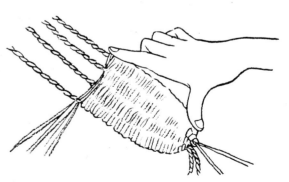

11. Continue weaving in an under-one/over-one pattern, adding rush as necessary. Pull the woven strands toward you with your left hand to tighten the weave. The width of the warp strands will be the width of the finished slipper, so be sure to keep the warp strands far enough apart.

12. Continue weaving up to where the thong is to be attached. The length from the heel to where the toes begin is usually about the span between the thumb and index finger when extended.

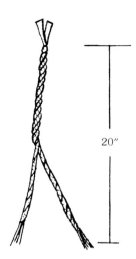 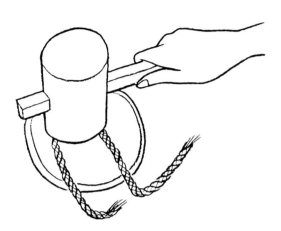

13. For the thong, wrap six or eight rush stems with the strip of fabric until you have covered about 20″ (51 cm). Make another wrapped strand. Tie the ends of the strands and twine them together into a cord for a thong (see Project 10).

14. Beat the thong with a wooden mallet to soften it.

15. Use the template to estimate how long the thong should be. There should be about 1¼″ (3.2 cm) between the nose of the slipper and the thong. The thong is attached in the middle of the slipper.

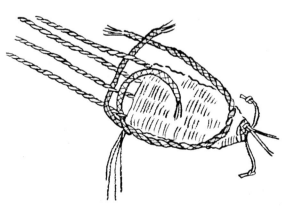 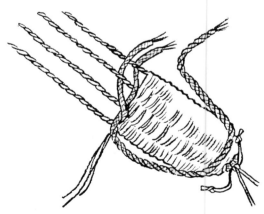

16. Leave the bunch of weaving strands to the side while you attach the thong. Untwine one end of the thong. Weave in one of the two wrapped strands of the thong.

17. Weave the other wrapped strand in, alternating under-one/over-one with the first strand. Leave the ends of the wrapped strands to the sides of the slipper.

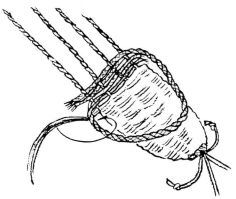

18. Repeat steps 16 and 17 with the other end of the thong. When resuming weaving with the bunch of rush, wrap it around the thong and weave across to secure the thong.

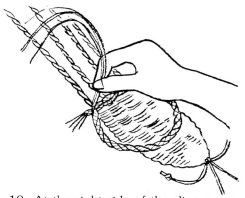

19. At the right side of the slipper, wrap the soft rush around the thong and continue weaving.

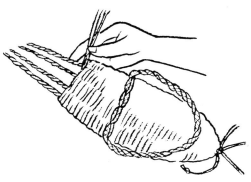

20. Gradually narrow the distance between the warp strands as you near the end.

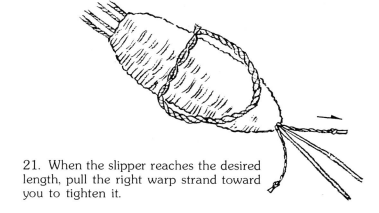

21. When the slipper reaches the desired length, pull the right warp strand toward you to tighten it.

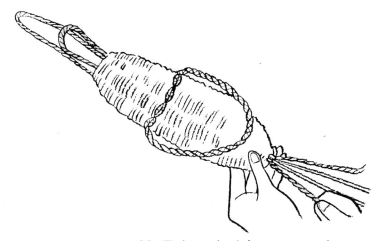

22. Tighten the left warp strand.

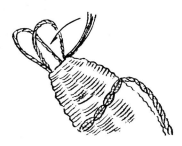

23. Take the warp strands off your toes or the weaving stand. Slip the end of the bunch of rush to the back through one of the warp strands and tighten the warp strands by pulling on the two center front strands.

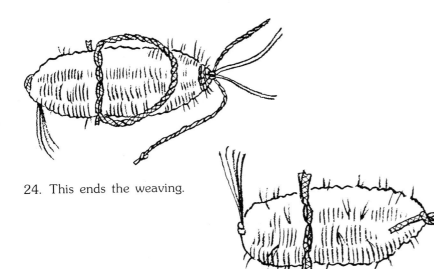

24. This ends the weaving.

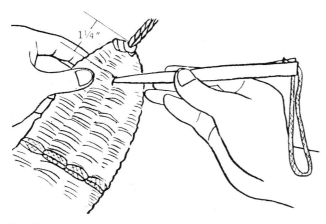

25. Turn the slipper over. Clip off the ends of the rush and wrapped strands, leaving the two strands at the nose.

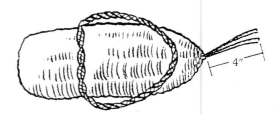

26. Cut off all but 4" (10 cm) of the warp strands.

27. Wrap three strands of rush with fabric strips until you have covered 15" (38 cm). Make another wrapped strand and twine the two together (see Project 10). Insert both ends of the twine in the guiding needle (see Project 14, step 23, page 92). With the sole of the slipper toward you, insert the guiding needle in the center, 1¼" (3.2 cm) from the nose.

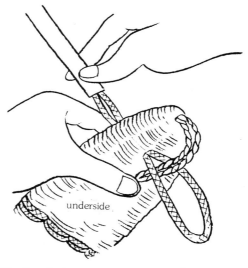

underside

28. Bend the two warp strands to the back and let them be caught in the loop of fabric-covered twine. Firmly pull the twine to the front.

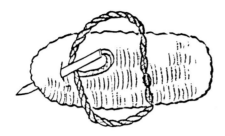

29. On the other side of the slipper, stitch over the center of the thong and pull the twine through to the back.

30. The thong is fastened to the woven part of the slipper by the thinner wrapped twine. Leave about ½" (1.3 cm) between the thong and the woven part so there is ample room for your foot.

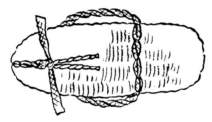

31. Turn the slipper over, and tie both ends of the fabric-wrapped twine around the warp strands. Cut off the ends.

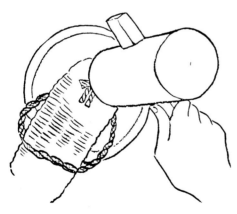

32. To flatten the knot, beat it with a wooden mallet. Repeat from step 4 for the other half of the pair. Note that there is no right or left to grass slippers.

ANOTHER ASPECT OF TRADITIONAL TECHNIQUES

The work of a highly trained traditional craftsman never fails to impress me with its intricacy and to make me respect the craftsman's command of technique. But at the same time, I feel the satisfaction he gets from technical mastery keeps him from venturing beyond the boundaries of tradition and developing other methods and values. Often such a craftsman's approach to creativity is to produce technical modifications of conventional schemes, which sometimes results in the display of technical prowess overwhelming the work itself.

Although this approach can create new forms, I think there are other creative possibilities. More potential for expression lies in each individual's pursuit of a new relation between himself and traditional techniques.

Studying primitive country crafts is a good way to develop insight into the harmonious relation between man and technology. Duplicating country crafts is not, of course, creative in itself, but their relative simplicity makes it easy to see how the relationship works.

The next four projects, besides bringing a bit of Japanese country life to your home, will help you visualize this relationship and understand how man has used fiber and developed ideas.

20

A STRING OF PEPPERS

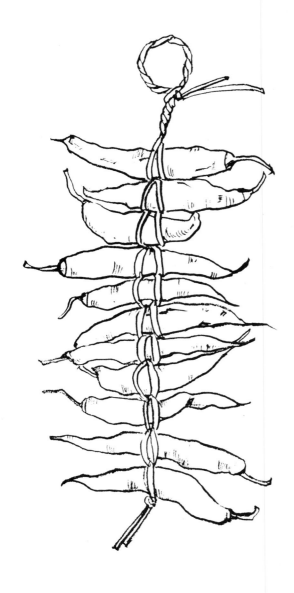

Many foods—long, white daikon radishes for pickles, small fish, and freeze-dried tofu—are strung and hung to dry under the eaves of farmhouses in the countryside of Japan.

MATERIALS

12″ (30 cm) soft rush, 4 stems
  Moisten.
  SUBSTITUTES: grasses like rice straw

⅜″ (1 cm) × 4″ (10 cm) dried red peppers (*aka-togarashi*), 11 peppers

FINISHED SIZE: H 8½″ (22 cm) × W 4″ (10 cm).

EQUIPMENT

Flower arrangement shears
T-pin
Board

INSTRUCTIONS

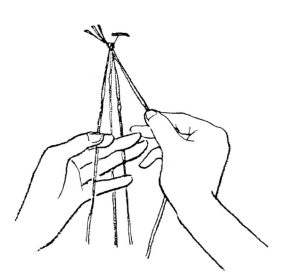

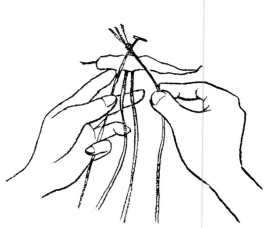

1. Tie the rush stems together near the end and pin the knotted end on a board.

2. Lift up a pair of stems and place the first red pepper sideways between the upper and lower pairs of stems and near the knot. Separate the stems of the upper pair and lay them down. Lift up the lower pair of stems.

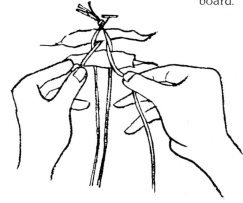

3. Slip the second pepper between the new upper and lower pairs. This simple movement makes two rows of vertical twining at the same time.

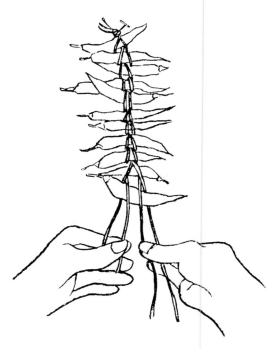

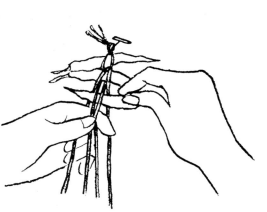

4. Repeat steps 2 and 3 until all the peppers have been strung. Pull on the stems from time to time to tighten the twining.

5. Separate the upper and lower pairs by picking up two stems in each hand: one from the upper pair and the other from the lower pair.

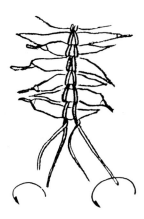

6. To make a strand of twine with the pairs of stems, twist each pair counterclockwise.

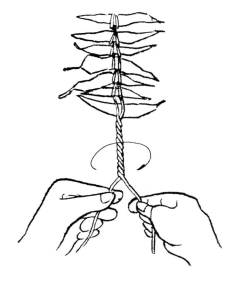

7. Twist the two pairs together clockwise.

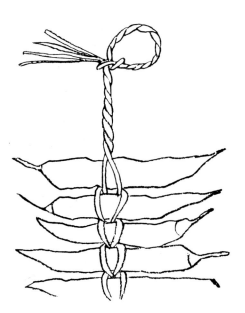

8. Loop and knot the strand of twine.

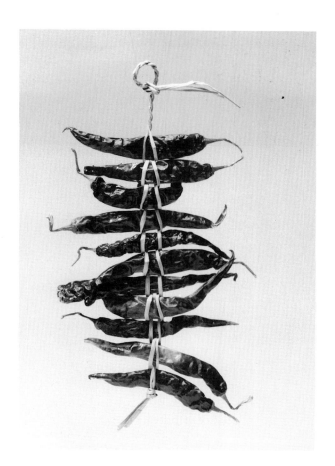

21

RICE CAKES WRAPPED IN DWARF BAMBOO LEAVES

The leaves of dwarf bamboo, *sasa*, a kind of broad-leafed, small bamboo, are known to contain a germicide. In Japan, these leaves are used in a traditional and natural wrapping that helps keep the food fresh. These sweetened rice cakes wrapped in bamboo leaves are called *chimaki* and are associated with Children's Day (May 5), and other holidays.

MATERIALS
⅔ cup (100 gm) rice flour (*mochi-ko*)
½ cup (100 gm) sugar
⅓ (80 cc) water

This makes 9 rice cakes.

Dwarf bamboo leaves
   27 wide leaves with stems attached (3 for each cake)

24" (60 cm) soft rush, 12   stems

FINISHED SIZE: 12" (30 cm)

EQUIPMENT
Mixing bowl
Cheesecloth
Steamer
Wooden spoon
Flower arrangement shears

INSTRUCTIONS

1. Mix the rice flour, sugar, and water in a bowl with your fingers until the mixture forms a sticky ball.

2. Wrap the ball in cheesecloth and steam it for 20 minutes.

3. Knead the hot steamed mixture with a wooden spoon until it becomes smooth.

4. When the mixture has cooled, work it with your hands until it is very smooth.

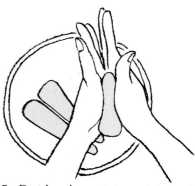

5. Divide the mixture into nine parts. Roll each part between the palms of your hands until the cake is shaped like a carrot.

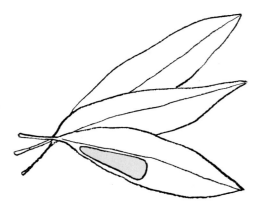

6. Lay three dwarf bamboo leaves back side up in a fan shape. The stem ends should overlap. Place a cake on the left end of the nearest leaf, tapered end to the left.

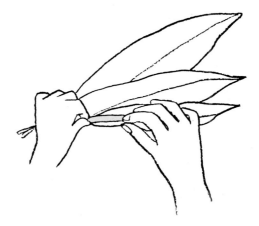

7. Roll the cake and leaves away from you.

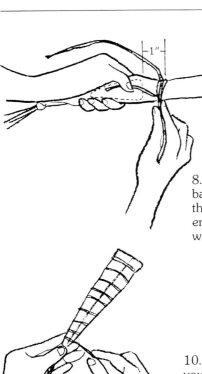

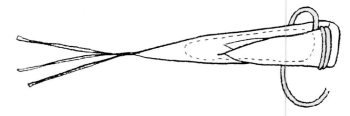

8. Wind a rush stem around the dwarf bamboo leaves 1″ (2.5 cm) to the right of the large end of the cake. Hold the short end of the rush under your left thumb and wind around the leaves twice.

9. Bend the leaf wrapping on the right of the rice cake to the left. The area wound with rush should now be on top. Continue winding the rush around the wrapping. The central vein of the leaf should be kept in the middle of the wrapping.

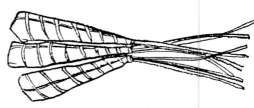

10. Continue winding the rush until you reach the stems of the dwarf bamboo leaves. Flip it over and cut the rush stem short, and tuck the cut end under the wound rush.

11. Repeat steps 6 through 10 twice.

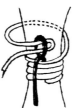

12. Tie the three wrapped packages together with a rush stem. Hold one end of the stem down so it lies with the leaf stems. Wrap the rush counterclockwise around the stems and over itself. Bring the stem of rush that is in the stems down to form a loop. Twist the loop. Form a loop with the other end and slip it through the twisted loop. Pull on this loop and the loose end of the twisted loop to tighten. This knot can be loosened with one tug, making it easy to open the package to eat the rice cakes.

22

PROTECTIVE SNOW CAP
FOR PLANTS

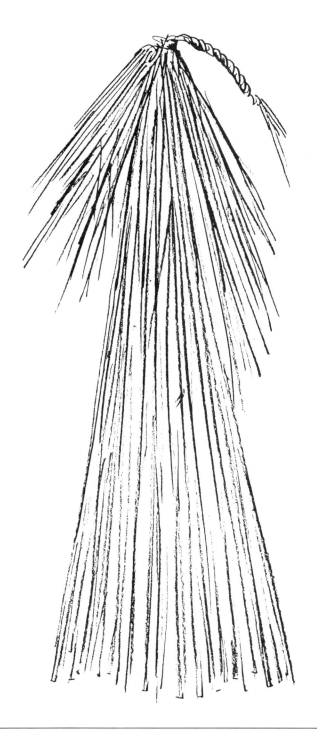

This simple bundle protects young plants like peonies from the snow and cold. Traditionally rice straw is used but any slender grass that is stiff enough to support itself but flexible enough to be bent can be substituted.

MATERIALS
3½ oz (100 gm) of 32" (80 cm) grass stems of the genus *Sporobolus*
Collect the grasses when they are mature and dry them. Moisten with an atomizer.
SUBSTITUTES: sedges, rushes

18" (46 cm) soft rush, 4 stems

FINISHED SIZE: H 21½" (55 cm) × D 11½" (29.3 cm)

EQUIPMENT
String
Atomizer

INSTRUCTIONS

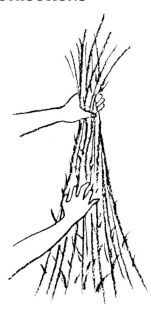

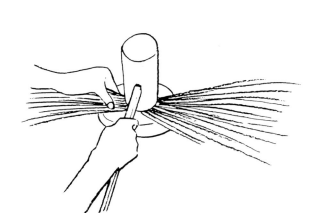

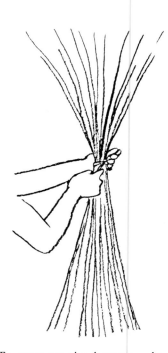

1. Spray the grasses with water to moisten. Remove any leaves from the stems by holding the grasses, tips up, in a bundle and raking down with your fingers.

2. To soften the fiber so it can be bent, pound the bundle with a wooden mallet slightly above the midpoint.

3. To even up the bottom edge of the snow cap, hold the bundle lightly and shake it up and down until all the butt ends of the stems touch the table. Make twine with the four strands of rush (see Project 10). Bind the area softened in step 2 with the twined rush. The upper part of the bundle will be the top of the snow cap.

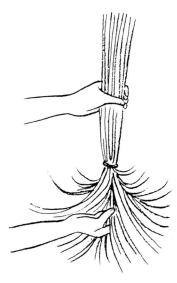

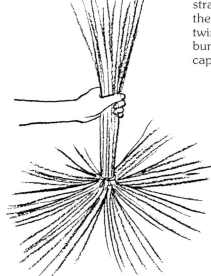

4. Turn the snow cap upside down. Hold the bundle in your left hand and press the tips of the grasses against the table while spreading them out with your right hand.

5. All the stems should radiate from the bound area evenly. The tips of the grass stems will be turned toward the butt end of the stems as they are twined around the bound area.

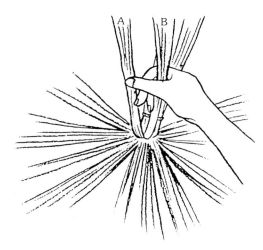

6. To begin twining around the bundle, pick up two small bundles of several stems each as shown.

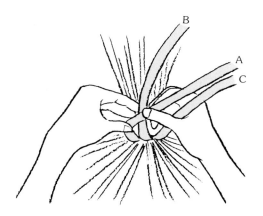

7. Bend the left bundle **A** over the right bundle **B** about 1" (2.5 cm) from the bound area. Pick up a new bundle **C** from the stems to the right of **A** and **B**.

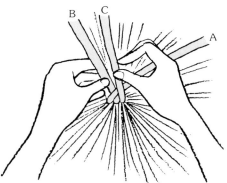

8. Lay the new bundle **C** over **A**.

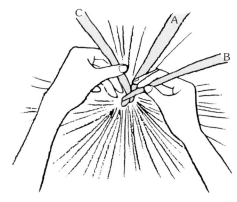

9. Bend **B** to the front over **C** and **A**. **A** should now be pointing in the same direction as the butt end of the stems.

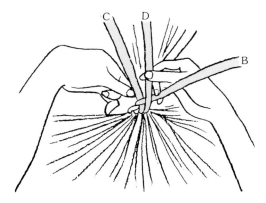

10. Pick up a new bundle **D** and bend it over **B**. Bend **C** to the front over **D** and **B**. **B** should now be pointing in the same direction as the butt end of the stems.

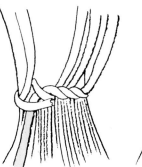

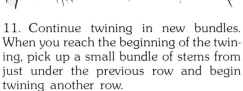

11. Continue twining in new bundles. When you reach the beginning of the twining, pick up a small bundle of stems from just under the previous row and begin twining another row.

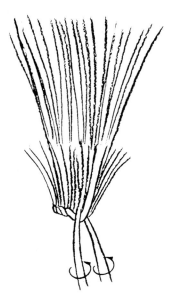

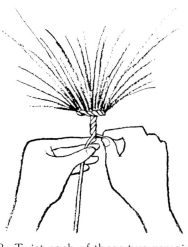

12. End the row of twining, leaving two untwined bundles of stems.

13. Twist each of these two remaining bundles counterclockwise, then twist them together clockwise as you do when making twine. Leave the very tips of the bundles untwined. This step secures the twinelike band made in the previous steps.

14. Flip the snow cap over and bend the twined tassel downward.

15. Open the lower part.

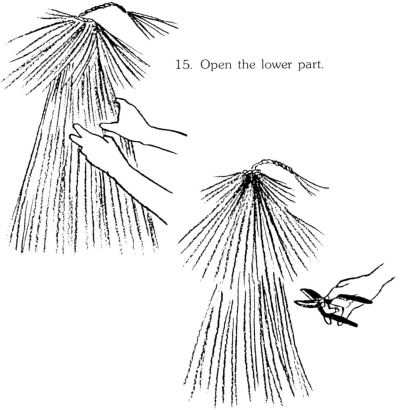

16. Trim the tips of the stems so they are roughly even.

23

WRAPPED EGGS

Although this traditional wrapping, usually made from rice straw, is not an independent basket, it is an interesting fiber structure. What is appealing about this simple package is the careful consideration given to matching the wrapping material and method to the five eggs to be wrapped. Five is a typical number for a set.

MATERIALS
Tule stems
    FOR WRAPPING THE EGGS: 20″ (51 cm), 25 stems
    FOR BINDERS: 24″ (60 cm), 6 stems
    Moisten.

5 eggs (you may use hard-boiled)

FINISHED SIZE: 2½″ (6.5 cm) × 10″ (25.5 cm)

EQUIPMENT
Flower arrangement shears
Atomizer

INSTRUCTIONS

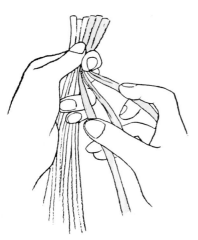

1. Make a bunch out of the 20" (51 cm) tule stems. Grasp the bunch near the top with your left hand, and lift up three strands with your right hand.

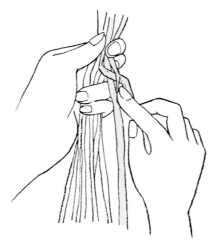

2. Braid these three strands until you have 2" (5 cm) of braid.

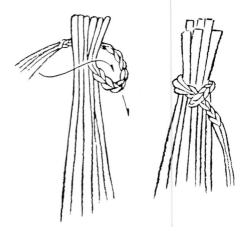

3. Tie the three-strand braid around the top of the bunch to bind it.

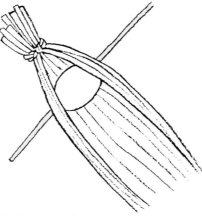

4. Spread the tule stems out to make a boat-shaped cavity. Slip the first binder under the bunch and place the egg on the tule stems horizontally.

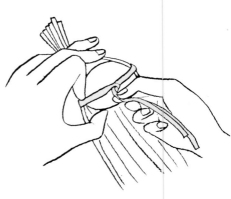

5. Twist the two ends of the binder together clockwise on top of the egg.

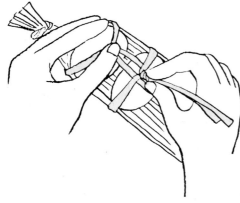

6. Hold the twist with your left thumb. Place the binder and second egg as in step 4. Twist the binder over the egg and the two ends of the first binder.

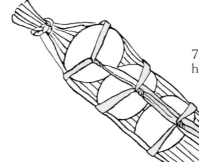

7. Repeat step 6 until all the eggs have been wrapped.

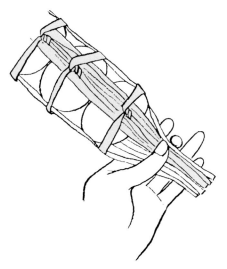

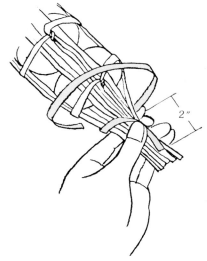

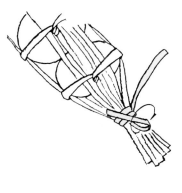

8. Gather the ends of all the binders and tule stems and hold them with your left hand.

9. Hold one end of the final binder under your left thumb at a point 2" (5 cm) from its cut end. Wind the other end of the binder counterclockwise around the bundle and over itself twice.

10. Lift up the end under the strand and lay it over the wound binder, forming a loop.

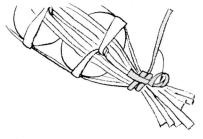

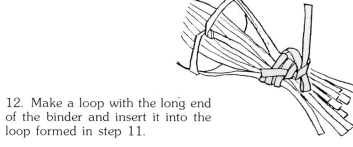

11. Twist the loop to the right.

12. Make a loop with the long end of the binder and insert it into the loop formed in step 11.

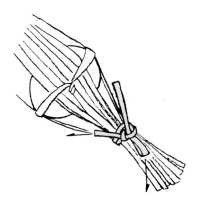

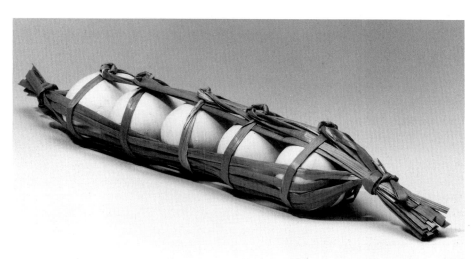

13. Pull the short end of the binder and the loop to tighten the knot.

PERSONAL INTEREST IN SOURCES OF MATERIAL

It was in 1979 that I first became really aware of how I got the materials for my baskets although I had already started to collect materials from the wild after studying with artists Sandra Newman and John McQueen and reading Carol Hart's book. I realize now my interest in the source of materials has given more dimension to my basketmaking. Through the collection of materials, I cannot help but be more aware of my environment. This turns my eyes to nature, to the season, to the society, and back to myself in the midst of all this.

In the middle of April that year, my friend was kind enough to let me know that she had found a box of pussy willows discarded in the flower district in New York. They were thrown away because there were too few buds on them. I wove them in a ti-twined open-work basket so the tips of the branches could be seen. The delight that came from using materials collected in this way was quite different from what I had felt before. This experience took on added significance for me when I heard artist Carol Westfall at Florence Duhl Gallery remark on her concern about sources for the city basketmaker's materials. After this, I started to pay more attention to how I got my materials.

I had another memorable experience after I came back to Japan. A report from a friend took me to downtown Tokyo to get some willow bark. Several pieces cut from the trunk of an old willow tree lay near heavy traffic, covered with mud and city soot. I was reluctant to touch them at first, the scene was so cruel and sad. But my feeling of shock vanished in a moment when I removed the stained, dirty outer bark and found that the sensuously wet, sweet, and white insides typical of the willow were unharmed. Tears welled up in my eyes when I saw how part of nature had struggled to remain unchanged even in such a tough environment. After I took the willow home, I scrubbed the outer bark with a brush—but not too thoroughly because I had decided to use the stained cracks on the corky surface as a pattern in a basket. I hoped the stains would look like a tattoo on the bark of the willow.

These two experiences led me to feel that beautiful and healthy materials from the remote countryside are not necessarily the best materials for me. These "finds" seemed more natural for someone who dwells in the crowded city. I have learned to value other features besides the visual quality of the material because I realize that those other features motivate my design in a different way and influence more significantly my philosophy of basketmaking.

It sounds naturalistic and romantic to make baskets out of materials you have collected in the wild. But if this cannot be part of your lifestyle, your basketmaking becomes unnatural and meaningless. Collecting your own materials is important not because it gives you a do-it-yourself feeling but because it is a way to express yourself. Therefore, the material should have some personal meaning for you. I will never forget how strongly John McQueen, in his workshop, emphasized that he keeps his rule of collecting all his own materials.

Nowadays, I collect willows trimmed from the Ginza in Tokyo, yucca leaves from parks, dracaena raised in my parents' garden, and all kinds of plants that are to be discarded. I have wisteria, mulberry, iris, ginger, black bamboo, and akebia in my very small backyard. My basket hot line with kind, sharp-eyed friends is of course a very precious human resource. I hope you will establish your own sources of materials and that your baskets will become a reflection of your personality and lifestyle.

For Your Reference

TOOLS

This Eastern European folk painting shows a basketmaker at work on a large wicker basket surrounded by his fundamental tools: a hatchet and saw to cut a tree or branches, a bodkin or awl, and a knife to thin or sharpen the ends of twigs. As this painting shows, generally speaking, basketmaking does not require many tools. I have listed what I usually use, but they are all tools I have "borrowed," changing their original functions to suit my own purpose. Therefore, once you understand their purpose, substitute appropriate tools from those readily at hand.

From the collection of Illy Valyi.

1. Bamboo split knife, 20 centimeters long, with double-edged, steel blade: Used for making anything from a rough split to delicate thinning, scraping outer bark, shaving splints, and sharpening ends. (Suggestions for substitution: thick blade hunting knife, draw knife.)
2. Saw: Used for cutting branches.
3. Buck knife.
4. Small, single-edged, steel knife called *kogatana*: Used for light cutting.
5. Needle-nosed pliers: Used to pinch material to soften the fiber at a corner or to pull with.
6. Alcohol burner: Used to heat twigs or splits to make them bendable and to burn off the hairy, feathered ends of fibers.
7. Embroidery scissors: Used for the finishing cut for fine fibers.
8. Swiss army knife: A narrow, double-edged knife for delicate tasks.
9. Various sizes of yarn needles: Used to stitch or to guide fiber through holes.
10. Flower arrangement shears.
11. Awl: Used to make space.
12. Bonsai trimming shears: Used to reach back corners.
13. Gardening shears: Used for heavy duty cutting.
14. Small wood-carving chisel: Used to scrape out the pithy core from a split vine or for whittling.
15. Hammer: Used to drive nails.
16. Atomizer: Used to moisten materials.
17. Wooden base and mallet: Used to beat fiber to soften it.
18. Piece of leather and heavy canvas: Used to protect the thigh when scraping.
19. Various fasteners: Used for temporary fastening and holding.

When other special devices are used, they are described in the projects.

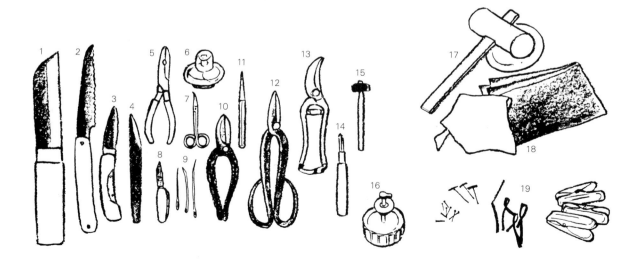

PLACES TO SEE BASKETS

This is not meant to be a comprehensive list, but simply places I have visited.

American Indian Archaeological Institute, Route 199 (Box 260), Washington, Connecticut 06793. (203) 868–0518

American Museum of Natural History, 79th Street and Central Park West, New York, New York 10024. (212) 873–1300
American aboriginal baskets and baskets of the world.

Bernice P. Bishop Museum, Honolulu, Hawaii.
South Pacific ethnological collection.

Chido Museum (Chido Hakubutsukan), 10–18 Kachu Shinmachi, Tsuruoka-shi, Yamagata-ken. (0235) 22–1199
Folk utensils of northern Japan.

Fuji Bamboo Garden (Fuji Takerui Shokubutsuen), 885 Minami Ishiki, Nagaizumi-cho, Sunto-gun, Shizuoka. (0559) 87–5498
Collection of bamboo. Museum.

Hancock Shaker Museum, Route 20, Pittsfield, Massachusetts 02101. (413) 443–0188

Heard Museum, 22 East Monte Vista Road, Phoenix, Arizona 85004. (602) 252–8848
American Indian basketry.

Japanese Farmhouse Museum (Nihon Minkaen), 7–1–1 Masugata, Tama-ku, Kawasaki-shi, Kanagawa-ken. (044) 922–2181
Open-air museum of 20 old farmhouses with dairy utensils.

Japan Folk Art Museum (Nihon Mingeikan), 4–3–33 Komaba, Meguro-ku, Tokyo (03) 467–4527
Folk art collection.

Kanko Bunka Kenkyujo, 73 Kanda Renpeicho, Chiyoda-ku, Tokyo. (03) 253–3485
Folk utensils. Library. Travel information. Open by appointment only.

Lyon Arboretum Association, 3860 D. Monoa Road, Honolulu, Hawaii.
Tropical botanical garden.

Musashino Art University (Musashino Bijutsu Daigaku), 1–736 Ogawa-cho, Kodaira-shi, Tokyo. (0423) 41–5011
Folk utensils. Not open to the public.

Museum of the American Indian, 155th Street and Broadway, New York, New York 10032. (212) 283–2420.

National Museum of Ethnology (Kokuritsu Minzokugaku Hakubutsukan), 10–1 Senri Banpaku Koen, Suita-shi, Osaka. (06) 876–2151

National Museum of Natural History, Smithsonian Institute, 10th Street and Constitution Avenue, N. W. Washington, D. C. 20560. (202) 357–1300
American aboriginal basketry and basketry of the world.

Nihon Jomin Bunka Kenkyujo, Kanagawa University, 3–27–1 Rokkakubashi, Kanagawa-ku, Yokohama-shi, Kanagawa-ken. (045) 481-5661
Old documents and publications. Not open to the public.

Numazu Rekishiminzoku Shiryokan, 2802–1 Shimokanuki-togo, Numazu-shi, Shizuoka. (0559) 32–6266
Collection of fishing equipment.

Oakland Museum, 1000 Oak Street, Oakland, California 94607. (415) 273–3402/3842.
American Indian baskets.

Peabody Museum of Archaeology and Ethnology, Harvard University, 11 Divinity Ave., Cambridge, Massachusetts 02138.
American Indian baskets.

Robert H. Lowie Museum of Anthropology, University of California, Berkeley, California.
Baskets of the world.

Shaker Museum, Old Chatham, New York 12136. (518) 749–9100
Colonial baskets and tools.

Tenri Sankokan, 1 Furu, Tenri-shi, Nara-ken. (07436) 3–1511
Ethnological collection.

The Textile Museum, 2320 S. Street. N. W. Washington, D. C. 20008.
Library.

University Museum of Pennsylvania, 33 and Spruce Street, Philadelphia, Pennsylvania 19174. (215) 898–4000
Ethnological collection.

Yokosuka City Museum (Yokosuka-shi Hakubutsukan), 95 Fukadadai, Yokosuka-shi, Kanagawa-ken. (0468) 24–3688
Collection of fishing nets, boats, other equipment.

Zenkoku Dentoteki Kogeihin Center, Plaza 246 2F, 3–1–1 Minami-Aoyama, Minato-ku, Tokyo. (03) 403–2460
Books and videos on the traditional craft industry.

SELECTED PUBLICATIONS

Adovasio, J. M. *Basketry Technology: A Guide to Identification and Analysis.* Chicago: Aldine Publishing Co., 1977.

Bager, Bertel. *Nature as Designer: A Botanical Art Study.* New York: Van Nostrand Reinhold, 1976.

Bell, Lillian. *Plant Fibers for Papermaking.* McMinnville, Oregon: Liliaceae Press, 1981.

Bobart, H. H. *Basketwork through the Ages.* London: Oxford University Press, 1936; Detroit: Singing Tree Press, Book Tower, 1971.

Brandford, Joanne Segal. *From the Tree Where the Bark Grows.* North American Basket Treasures from the Peabody Museum, Harvard University. Cambridge: New England Foundation for the Arts, 1984.

Brigham, T. William and Hon. John F. G. Stokes. *Mat and Basket Weaving of the Ancient Hawaiians.* Memoirs of the Bernice P. Bishop Museum, vol. 2. 1906–09. Reprint. New York: Kraus Reprint Co., 1974.

Britton, Nathaniel L., and Hon. Addison Brown. *An Illustrated Flora of the Northern United States and Canada.* 3 vols. New York: Charles Scribner, 1913; New York: Dover Publishing Co., 1970.

Brown, Lauren. *Grasses: An Identification Guide.* Boston: The Peterson Nature Library, 1979.

Buck, Peter H. *Arts and Crafts of Cook Island.* Bishop Museum Bulletin no. 179. 1904. Reprint. New York: Kraus Reprint Co., 1971.

——. *Arts and Crafts of Hawaii.* Bishop Museum Bulletin no. 45, sections 3,4. 1957. Reprint. New York: Kraus Reprint Co., 1964.

Constantine, Mildred, and Jack L. Larsen. *Art Fabric: The Mainstream.* New York: Van Nostrand Reinhold, 1981.

Diamonstein, Barbaralee. *Handmade in America.* New York: Harry N. Abrams, Inc., 1983.

Dye Plants and Dyeing, Vol. 20, No. 3. 3rd ed. New York: Brooklyn Botanic Garden, 1976.

Edwards, Ron. *Australian Traditional Bush Crafts.* New York: Schochen Books, 1977.

Emery, Irene. *Primary Structures of the Fabrics.* 2nd ed. Washington, D. C.: Textile Museum, 1966.

Handy, Willowdean C. *Handicrafts of the Society Island.* Bishop Museum Bulletin no. 42. 1927. Reprint. New York: Kraus Reprint Co., 1971.

Hart, Carol G. *Natural Basketry.* New York: Watson-Guptill, 1976.

Hayashi, Yasaka, Kazuo Furusato, and Tsuneo Nakamura, eds. *Illustrated Trees in Color.* Tokyo: Hokuryukan, 1985.

James, G. Warton. *Indian Basketry.* 1909. Reprint. New York: Dover Publications, 1975.

Jones, Suzi. *Pacific Basket Makers: A Living Tradition.* A catalogue of the 1981 Pacific Basketmaker's Symposium and Exhibition. Fairbanks, Alaska: University of Alaska Museum, 1981.

Kayano, Shigeru. *Ainu no mingu.* Tokyo: Suzusawa Shoten, 1978.

Kihara, Yoshijiro, and Hikonojo Nakahara. *Seni shokubutsu.* Tokyo: Kyoritsu Shuppan, 1942.

Knobel, Edward. *Field Guide to the Grasses, Sedges, and Rushes of the United States.* New York: Dover Publications, 1977.

Kobayashi, Yukio. *Zoku kodai no gijutsu.* Tokyo: Hanawa Shobo, 1983.

Kondo, Kyoji. *Higashinippon-hen.* Mingei no tabi. Tokyo: Unsodo, 1978.

Kraus, Beatrice H. *Ethnobotany of Hawaii.* Honolulu: University of Hawaii, 1980.

Kudo, Kazuyoshi. *Japanese Bamboo Baskets.* Tokyo: Kodansha International, 1980.

Kuoni, Bignia. *Cesteria Tradicional Iberica.* Barcelona: Ediciones del Serbal, 1981.

Langsner, Drew. *Country Woodcraft.* Emmaus, Pennsylvania: Rodale Press, 1978.

Levinsohn, Rhoda. *Basketry: A Renaissance in Southern Africa.* Cleveland Heights, Ohio: Protea Press, 1979.

Makino, Tomitaro. *Makino's Illustrated Flora in Color.* Tokyo: Hokuryukan, 1985.

——. *Makino's Illustrated Pocket Book of Japanese Plants in Color.* Tokyo: Hokuryukan, 1985.

——. *New Illustrated Flora of Japan.* Tokyo: Hokuryukan, 1961.

Mason, Otis T. *Aboriginal American Indian Basketry.* Smithsonian Institute Annual Report, 1904. Reprint. Santa Barbara: Peregrine Smith, Inc., 1976.

Mingu Seisaku Gijutsu Hozonkai. *Mingu no tsukurikata,* no. 1–18. Kawasaki: Mingu Seisaku Hozonkai, 1976–80.

Miyamoto, Tsuneichi. *Nippon no mingu.* Tokyo: Keiyusha, 1969.

Muroi, Hiroshi. *Take.* Tokyo: Hosei University Press, 1979.

Nakamura, Shunkichi. "Chubu chiho no takekago ni tsuite." Kokuritsu minzokugaku hakubutsukan kenkyu hokoku, vol. 2, no. 2: p. 351.

——. "Chugoku chiho no takekago ni tsuite." Kokuritsu minzokugaku hakubutsukan kenkyu hokoku, vol. 2, no. 4: p. 806.

——. "Kanto chiho no takekago ni tsuite." Kokuritsu minzokugaku hakubutsukan kenkyu hokoku, vol. 2, no. 1: p. 172.

——. "Kinki chiho no takekago ni tsuite." Kokuritsu minzokugaku hakubutsukan kenkyu hokoku, vol. 2, no. 3: p. 605.

——. "Nihon no makikago ni tsuite." Kokuritsu minzokugaku hakubutsukan kenkyu hokoku, vol. 4, no. 2: p. 340.

——. "Palawan, Borneo, Java, Sumatra no kago ni tsuite." Kokuritsu minzokugaku hakubutsukan kenkyu hokoku, vol. 4, no. 1: p. 130.

Nukata, Iwao. *Tsutsumi.* Tokyo: Hosei University Press, 1977.

Read, Herbert. *The Meaning of Art.* London: Farber & Farber, Ltd., 1949.

Rossbach, Ed. *Baskets as Textile Art.* New York: Van Nostrand Reinhold, 1973.

——. *The New Basketry.* New York: Van Nostrand Reinhold, 1976.

Rudofsky, Bernard. *Architecture Without Architects.* New York: Museum of Modern Art, 1964.

Sato, Shogoro. *Take kogei.* Tokyo: Kyoritsu Shuppan, 1974.

Sugiyama, Sueo. *Nippon genshi seni kogeishi.* 1942. Reprint. Hokkaido: Hokkaido Shuppan Kikaku, 1979.

Suzuki, Hisao. *Nishinihon-hen.* Mingei no tabi. Tokyo: Unsodo, 1979.

Thompson, Nile, and Carolyn Marr. *Crow's Shells: Artistic Basketry of Puget Sound.* Seattle: Dushuyay Publications, 1983.

Tod, Osma Gallinger. *Earth Basketry.* 1933. Reprint. Coral Gables, Florida: Osma Gallinger Tod Weaving Studio, n.d.

Uezu, Hitoshi, et al. *Ryuku shoto no mingu.* Tokyo: Miraisha, 1983.

Umezao, Tadao. *Bunmei no seitaishikan.* Tokyo: Chuokoronsha, 1967.

Will, Christoph. *International Basketry.* East Exton, Pennsylvania: Schiffer Publishing, 1985.

Wright, Dorothy. *The Complete Book of Baskets and Basketry.* New York: Scribners, 1977.

Yamazaki, Masakazu. *Konton kara no hyogen.* Kyoto: PHP, 1977.

INDEX

Aka-togarashi. See Red peppers
Akebia, 45, 47, 48, 140
Analysis of a Basket, 15—16

"Balanced V," 74
Bamboo, 46, 48
  splits, 88, 115
  stalk, 54
Bamboo Screen with Weighted Bobbin
  Twining, 54, 60, 107, 109, 115—118
Banana sheaths, 37
Basketry, 25, 96
  concepts, 67—76
  definition of, 10, 67
Baskets, African, 13
Baskets, American Indian, 13, 52
"Between Acts," 71
Birch, 52, 96
Braid, six-strand, 60. *See also* Cattail braid
Braiding, 60
Broussonetia papyrifera. See Paper mulberry

Camellia oil, 45
Cattail braid, 13, 97. *See also* Braid,
  six-strand
Cattail Braid and Maple Splint Basket, 57,
  60, 96, 97—100, 106—07
Cattails, 45, 46, 48, 60, 64, 75, 96, 97
Cedar, 45, 52
Century plant, Central American, 45
Chamaecyparis sp. bark, 74
Cherry bark, 17, 45, 48, 68, 69, 74, 75, 76,
  88, 109
Children's Day, 130
Chimaki, 130
Coiled Basket, 33—36, 42, 96
Coiling, 11, 12, 14, 34
Coiling, short-strand, 96, 101—04
Corn husk mat. *See* Short-Strand Coiled
  Mat
Corn husks, 101
Crafts, traditional Japanese, 126
"Cut and Opened Hull," 13, 14, 71

Dwarf bamboo leaves, 45, 48, 130
Dyeing with Onion Skins, 45, 65—66

Egg white and rice starch adhesive, 45
"Even a Basket Rusts," 76

Fiber plants, 44
Fish trap, 15

Grass, 45, 97, 119
Grass Slippers, 60, 107, 109, 119—25
Guiding needle, 88, 92, 109, 119

Hanging Basket Made from Windmill Palm
  Stem, 78, 79—81, 105

Hanging Basket with Curved Bottom, 82,
  83—87, 105
"Hexagonal Openwork Basket," 76
"Hollow Solidity," 74
How To Make Twine and Braid, 37, 45,
  60—64, 97
How To Prepare Cherry Bark, 45, 52—53
How To Prepare Paper Mulberry Bark, 45,
  50—51
How To Split a Maple Log, 44, 45, 57—59
How To Split Bamboo Stalks, 44, 54—56

Imbrication, 13, 14, 52
"Indented," 13, 14, 75
Interaction of materials and methods, 48—49
Interplay of form, material, and method, 8,
  9, 10
Iris, 70, 97

Japanese kudzu, 45
Japanese splint basket, 13, 14
Japanese Winnowing Basket, 50, 52, 54, 82,
  88—95, 105
Juncus effusus, 60, 119. *See also* Soft rush
Jute, 45, 60

Kaki shibu, 45
Knotting, 11, 12, 14, 16

"Lines with Width and Depth," 72
Livistona, 78
Looping, 11, 12, 14, 16

McQueen, John, 8, 109, 140
Maple, 45, 47, 48, 57
Maple splints, 13, 75, 88, 96, 97
Maquette, 109
Material, 8, 9
  properties of, 10, 44—45, 69
  preparation of, 44—45
Methods, 10, 11, 69
  basic, 11, 12, 14, 15, 16
Mulberry, 50
  bark, 68, 69, 74, 88
  shoots, 88

Netted bait sinker, 13, 14
Newman, Sandra, 140

Paper mulberry, 46, 48, 73
Persimmon juice, 45
Peter's Valley Craft Center, 8, 109
Plaited Basket, 37—41, 42—43, 60
Plaited Basket in a Free-Form Willow Basket,
  106, 109, 110—14
Plaiting, 11, 12, 14, 16, 110
Pomo Indians, 25
Protective Snow Cap for Plants, 44, 108,
  133—36

Raffia, 65
Ramie, 37, 47, 60, 63
Rattan. *See* Round reed
Red peppers, 127
Rice Cakes Wrapped in Dwarf Bamboo
  Leaves, 108, 130—32
Rice straw, 45, 48, 61, 96, 119, 127, 133
Rossbach, Ed, 8
Round reed, 17, 25, 33, 70, 76, 79
Rush, 45, 48, 60. *See also* Soft rush

Sasa. See Dwarf bamboo leaves
"Sashed Space," 70
Shimenawa, 115
Shinodake, 54, 74
Short-Strand Coiled Mat, 96, 101—04,
  106—07
Sinomenine, 47, 70, 71, 75, 83, 97
"Slits from Scars," 68
Soft rush, 61, 119, 127, 130. *See also* Rush
Space as tangible material, 8, 67, 82
"Space Encircled Space," 70
"Squarely Wrapped," 75
String of Peppers, A, 108, 127—29
Structural characteristics, 11, 14

Technique. *See* Methods
Tegokoro, 83
Textile technology, 10
Ti, 25
Ti-twining, 27—31
Tools, 44, 141
Transformational factors, 12, 14, 15, 16
Tule, 119, 137
Twine, 37, 41, 60, 73
"Twine-Bound Space," 73
Twined Openwork Basket, 25—32, 43
Twining, 11, 12, 13, 14, 16
  three-strand, 20
  with weighted bobbins, 109, 115—18

Urushi lacquer, 45

Vegetable dye, 45, 65
Vegetable wax, 45

Washi, 45
Weaverbird, 10
Weaving, 11, 12, 14
Westfall, Carol, 140
White birch, 33, 48
Willow, 45, 46, 48, 70, 76, 96, 110
  bark, 72, 74, 110, 140
  branches, 72
  twigs, 25, 33
Windmill palm, 48, 78, 79
Wisteria, 45, 47, 48, 71, 140
Woven Basket, 17—24, 42, 52
Wrapped Eggs, 108, 137—39